To. Jeff.

Enjoy the Hit!

PETER CROKER'S
PATH TO BETTER GOLF

May this book help you
understand a little more about
this great game.
I thank you for your interest
& Professional support in bringing
my teachings to Vale.
Your assistant coach.

Peter Croker

March 2004

PETER CROKER'S

PATH TO BETTER GOLF

THE REVOLUTIONARY SWING TECHNIQUE FOR POWER, CONTROL, AND CONSISTENCY

PETER CROKER

HarperResource

An Imprint of HarperCollins*Publishers*

HarperCollins books may be purchased for educational, business, or sales promotional use. For information please write: Special Markets Department, HarperCollins Publishers, Inc., 10 East 53rd Street, New York, NY 10022.

FIRST EDITION

DESIGNED BY RENATO STANISIC

Library of Congress Cataloging-in-Publication Data

Croker, Peter.
    Peter Croker's path to better golf : the revolutionary swing technique for power, control, and consistency / Peter Croker.—1st ed.
        p. cm.
    Includes index.
    ISBN 0-06-019790-0
    1. Swing (Golf)   2. Golf.   I. Title: Path to better golf.   II. Title.

GV979.S9 C79 2002
796.352'3—dc21   2001024300

02 03 04 05 06   RRD   10 9 8 7 6 5 4 3 2 1

I dedicate this book to my children, Nikki and Ben; my parents, Norrie and Ruth; and my brothers, Douglas and Ian, together with their families, for all their support and encouragement during my search for a simpler way to teach and play golf. Also, to grassroots instructors all around the world who dedicate their lives to helping others improve at golf. I trust this text will provide them with a more workable and simple system of teaching, so that more and more amateur players can be put on the Path to Better Golf.

CONTENTS

ACKNOWLEDGMENTS

Putting this book together reminds me a lot about writing a play and then seeing it later performed on a Broadway stage. I guess what I am trying to say is that before I began this project I had no idea what a production it was going to become and how much work was involved. I also had no idea how exciting it would be seeing the finished product, for I knew that my hard work had paid off and a multitude of golfers would improve as a result of reading the book you now hold in your hands. I say that out of sheer pride for my diligent work, and not out of conceit. But I'm getting ahead of myself.

Long before ever thinking about writing *Path to Better Golf,* I spent years searching for the secrets to the swing— technical elements that the pros proved worked but never talked about, and tips I could pass on to recreational players.

That investigative process was no less than arduous and involved hundreds and hundreds of hours of analysis. Not only did I review the swings of amateurs to determine their common errors, I spent an equal amount of time examining the best players from the past and present, most notably the late Ben Hogan and Tiger Woods, who are featured in this book. I also consulted with many PGA and LPGA pros. Now, with the publication of *Path to Better Golf,* I owe them great thanks. The list is long and includes such notable names as Bill Adams, Debbie Austin, Denis Brosnan, Jason Eldering, Bryan Ferguson, Jim Ferree, Paul Hart, Randy Henry, Tim Ireland, David Iwasaki-Smith, Mal Jack, Lin Jacquelin, Sue Kaffenburgh-Thimme, John Kennedy, Andrew Mowatt, Simon Owen, Tim Poland, Paul Runyan, Tom Shea, Achim Steinfurth, Cindy Swift-Jones, Paul Moloney, Peter Thomson, and the late Homer Kelley. Other non-PGA members who were there to bounce ideas off of and broaden my understanding of the golf swing include Danny Acret, Mike Baker, Joel Barker, Lee Dietrich, Jeffrey Johnson, Michael Manavian, Fred Ost, Michael Pomerantz, Marten Runow, Tom Tomasello, Erik Wredenfors, and my family.

As to the actual publication of the book, I owe great thanks to my agent and editor John Andrisani, a former instruction editor of *GOLF Magazine* and renowned author who served as chief creative director on this project. I am also grateful to Matthew Benjamin, editor at HarperCollins, who believed in my methods of teaching and helped suggest better ways to get across the instructional messages contained in *Path to Better Golf.* The skills of these two professionals had a whole lot to do with the final production of this book, which I believe you will find enjoyable to read and very helpful.

Path to Better Golf has been greatly enhanced by the photographs and artwork that accompany the written text. For their input, I thank photographers Paul Nurnberg, Peter Turrell, and Jules Alexander. I'm also grateful to artist Shu Kuga, who modeled his illustrations of Ben Hogan on original photographs taken by Jules Alexander and did some wonderful paintings of Tiger Woods swinging. And I can't forget Gregory Bridges for his innovative illustrations showing me in action.

I could go on and on thanking the many persons who helped in this project. Numerous pages would be filled with names, and no matter how hard I tried I would inevitably leave someone off the list. Therefore, let me just say that I also thank those many individuals who know they were instrumental in helping me unravel the mysteries of the golf swing so that I could share what I have learned with you and others.

Good luck and work hard, because your progress is my most valued reward.

FOREWORD

I'm fifty-two years old and have been playing golf since I
was eight. When I first picked up a club, in 1957, golf was not
a booming sport. Back then even many private clubs lacked a
practice range. This is why the shag bag was a popular item.
Enthusiastic golfers, such as myself, used to empty a shag bag
of balls and hit them across a field or school grounds, then go
pick them up. On my way to retrieve them, I used to wonder
what it would be like to know the secret to the swing. I
couldn't even get this answer from any of the local pros since
they rarely gave lessons and were not interested in dissecting
the swing into components. The reason: very few club players
really took the game that seriously. It was just a sport that you
played on weekends.

Well, I took golf seriously. So much so that I eventually

turned professional in 1971 and started teaching golf. I read everything there was to read, including books by Arnold Palmer, Sam Snead, and Ben Hogan. However, the author of one of my favorite books, *Golf Isn't Hard*, is Australian Norman Von Nida. An uncle of mine gave me that book in 1959, when I was just ten. For some reason, probably because it is so simply written and features a number of photographs, I like to refer back to this text from time to time.

It's ironic that, forty plus years after receiving Von Nida's book, another Australian would have such a great influence on my golfing life. What made this happen? The story begins in 1978, when I changed careers and began writing about golf. I moved to England to work as an assistant editor at *Golf Illustrated* magazine, while at the same time doing freelance writing. While in England, I regained my amateur-golf status and played often. I particularly loved the courses in Surrey, such as Walton Heath, Hindhead, Woking, St. George's Hill, and Burhill. My biggest thrill was playing with pro Sandy Lyle, at his home club, Hawkstone Park in Shropshire, and shooting two under par 70 to his 68. It was the only time in my life I did not score a bogey during a round.

While in England, I belonged to the Plus-Four Society, open to players of four-handicap and below. I was a three-handicap at Home Park, located right near Hampton Court, one of King Henry VIII's former homes.

In 1982, I took a job as instruction editor for *GOLF Magazine,* in New York. Jumping ahead further, I stayed there until 1998, when I started concentrating on writing golf instruction books full-time.

During my long stint at *GOLF Magazine,* something

strange happened. Although I worked on articles with the greatest teachers in golf, including Jimmy Ballard, Hank Haney, Jim McLean, and Butch Harmon, and played with big-name pros—everybody from Seve Ballesteros to Curtis Strange, to Chichi Rodríguez—my handicap actually rose each year. In fact, when I left *GOLF Magazine,* my handicap was eight. Granted, at times a tip from an instructor or tour player helped me. But my game never returned to its old form. This was hard to take, and I did not think things would change. Every time I played I depended on different swing thoughts, different physical keys. Nothing turned me into a consistent player. Some days I played great, other days not so well. Most of the time during a round my driving game was in and out. My problems: I hit an occasional duck hook shot or slice shot that caused me to score double bogey or triple bogey on a hole and ruin my score. This was all to change in September 1999 when I took a lesson from Peter Croker. Before telling you about that lesson, I would like to introduce you to Croker, present proof of his professional credibility, and provide you with a crash-course glimpse into his teaching philosophies.

WHO IS PETER CROKER?

Croker is a former Australian tour player who in the late 1970s decided to devote his life to solving the mysteries of the golf swing.

Eventually, Croker discovered the secrets to consistently sending the ball powerfully along a designated flight path. At first, the largely unconventional principles that form the basis for Croker's Path to Better Golf theory were laughed at.

However, when Croker backed up his method with proof that the game's greatest golfers apply these very same principles for setting up and swinging, but for whatever reason never reveal them, many teachers who once considered Croker a rebel converted.

Whereas most teachers encourage students to swing the club, Croker teaches the art of *hitting* the ball. He believes that it's a much more free action, both physically and mentally. He's also quick to point out that, in doing his research, he discovered that golf's greatest player, Jack Nicklaus, was taught by Jack Grout, the pro at Scioto Golf Club in Ohio, to hit hard at the ball from the time he was a young boy. This fact helps support Croker's hit theory.

It doesn't hurt that some of the game's top teaching professionals now depend on Croker's methods to help recreational players make a more athletic, consistently powerful, and accurate swing. Furthermore, some of the PGA Tour's straightest hitters such as Fred Funk, and longest hitters such as Vijay Singh, have had their swings put on the correct path by Croker, whom they consider a genius.

The corporate world has a lot of confidence in Croker too, namely because he helps many Wall Street "players" score better and play more enjoyable golf. Croker often jets off to New York, Geneva, London, Frankfurt, Barcelona, and other major cities to teach the privileged privately or to conduct three-day corporate clinics for big bucks. Ironically, Croker also spends many hours a year giving free lessons to less fortunate youngsters around the United States. The bottom line: Croker instructs all types of individuals—old, young, men, women, children. In fact, his Path to Better Golf lessons have been taught in schoolyards, airplanes, gourmet restaurants, barbershops—you name it.

When in America, The Majors Golf Club in Palm Bay, Florida, and his other bases, Croker divides his time between helping average club golfers lower their handicap and teaching teachers his method as part of a certification program. And one thing is for sure, he knows what he's talking about, as the following endorsements attest.

Peter Croker's advice will help you improve your ball-striking and lower your scores.

—PETER THOMSON: FIVE-TIME BRITISH OPEN CHAMPION

I was skeptical at first about Peter Croker's instruction, namely because I'm a traditionalist. However, after weeks of watching and listening to Croker teach golf, I became a strong believer in his methods. The physics and geometric elements of the swing, which Croker explains so succinctly, are irrefutable.

—GARY SCHAAL: PAST PRESIDENT OF THE PGA OF AMERICA

After being introduced to Peter Croker and his method, I now feel that I am giving students at Yale the best possible information about their golf swings. The Path to Better Golf program and drills have made a significant change in students' improvement.

—PETER PULASKI: PGA PROFESSIONAL AND DIRECTOR OF GOLF
OPERATIONS OF YALE UNIVERSITY GOLF COURSE

Peter Croker's Path to Better Golf teaching method is biomechanically sound. It creates a golf swing that rotates nicely around the spine. Croker has correctly identified the proper sequence of movements in a good golf swing. His simple drills allow golfers to quickly learn these movements. In just one month after applying Croker's method I started hitting irons more crisply and longer and straighter than ever before. I believe I have found a golf swing that will last a lifetime.

—FRED DOAN: EXECUTIVE DIRECTOR OF THE
AMERICAN FLEXIBILITY INSTITUTE

Thanks to using Peter Croker's Path to Better Golf program, I became the proud recipient of the Teacher of the Year award among golf instructors.

—SANDY KURCEBA: MEMBER OF THE CANADIAN PGA

Peter Croker's Path to Better Golf is simple, educational, and beneficial to any golf instructor. It furthered my understanding of the golf swing, clarified questions about mechanics, and enhanced my communication skills as an instructor. My students now have a clear picture of what to do and consistently hit the ball with more structure, power, and control. Yes, they are playing better and having more fun. I thank Croker for taking my teaching skills to the next level and my students to the next generation of champions.

—GLEN DÉCK: PGA MEMBER AND 1996 TEACHER OF THE YEAR
IN THE SOUTHERN CALIFORNIA SECTION

Through years of experience as an accomplished player and acclaimed golf instructor, Peter Croker has founded a refresh-

ing new school of thinking in golf instruction, backed up by innovative drills to expedite the learning process.

—WILLIAM SAFRIN: EDUCATION CO-CHAIRMAN
OF THE NEW ENGLAND PGA

Peter Croker's Path to Better Golf teaching system enabled me to add twenty yards to my drive, and to hit long irons for the first time in my golfing life. Without Peter's help, I do not think I would have made the prestigious Walker Cup team.

—DUKE DELCHER: A TOP-NOTCH PLAYER WITH A BRIGHT FUTURE IN
AMATEUR GOLF

As an eighteen-year-old I finished fifth in the Italian Amateur Championship. As a nineteen-year-old, I won the Italian Amateur Matchplay Championship. Peter Croker's simple teaching methods are responsible for my improved play and power game. I'm only five feet five inches tall, yet I now hit tee shots 285 yards—and accurately!

—MICHAEL ROSSI: ONE OF EUROPE'S UP-AND-COMING PLAYERS

PETER CROKER'S ULTIMATE GOAL

The number of golfers is rapidly increasing, but players are not improving despite the technologically advanced equipment on the market. For this reason Croker believes golf instruction should be standardized, with his method taking precedence over all others. Croker's chief priority is to make the Path to Better Golf the standard method of teaching in the world. If that goal seems ambitious, one simple fact convinces Croker that it is not: his students improve.

The Path to Better Golf system of teaching is far removed

from the conventional swing methods. In creating his standardized system, Croker completely redefined instructional terminology, substituting old fundamentals with new fundamentals and popularizing words such as *push, throw,* and *hit.*

Croker's system is creating such a buzz that more and more PGA professionals—who have been searching for solid principles to pass on to their students—are now attending his "Teach the Teacher" training programs. The teacher's goal is to pass various tests and become qualified to teach the Push-Golf method, which is the foundation of Croker's Path to Better Golf system. Presently, instructors are teaching Croker's system in Australia, South Africa, Japan, England, Scotland, Switzerland, Germany, Spain, Austria, Puerto Rico, Singapore, Malaysia, India, Canada, and of course, the United States.

WHY IS THE MAN ONCE CONSIDERED A REBEL NOW CONSIDERED A RENAISSANCE MAN?

The answer is quite simple. Croker discovered a unique way of teaching golf and his theory was first presented to the golfing masses in April 1995 when *Golf Digest* magazine ran a cover story entitled "Your Swing of the Future."

On the cover of that issue, what's considered the world's finest golf publication ran the following blurb, with futuristic art showing Croker swinging into impact:

The new, Australian move promises:

- Solid contact
- A cure for your slice
- Instant results
- Less strain on your back

Golf Digest took a gamble with this cover story. Its credibility was on the line.

Croker had discovered that good golf is the result of a *pushing* action, not a pulling action, which is what amateur students around the world had previously been taught to believe. *Golf Digest* wanted to tell the golf world about this new method, believing it would cause a paradigm shift in instruction. They were so bullish about Croker's concept that they devoted ten pages to the story and had their managing editor, Roger Schiffman, coauthor the piece rather than instruction writer Guy Yocum. *Golf Digest's* gamble paid off. Not only was the issue a blockbuster on the newsstands, the magazine staff received thousands of letters from readers, thanking them for turning their game around.

MY LESSON

I felt comfortable being taught by Peter Croker. I knew him as a fine player and swing scholar. Right from the start of my two-hour-long lesson, he impressed me. He listened intently as I gave my impressions on the swing and its components and never took his eyes off me when I hit balls. He had me hit balls with the sand wedge first, and the driver, my most problematic club, second.

During our lesson, Croker did for me what no other teacher had ever done. He taught me the correct impact position before the address, because, as he explained, the main object of the swing is to be able to return the club squarely and powerfully into the ball. In describing impact, Croker was passionate, namely because he wanted me to understand that impact starts the moment the ball is struck, then continues on until the club travels several inches forward and the right arm straightens. Moreover, contrary to popular belief among golfers, the right arm does not straighten until after the ball is struck, and far more weight is on the right foot, not the left foot, when the club meets the ball. Just these two revelations about impact helped me time the swing better and hit the ball more powerfully and accurately virtually automatically. Pushing the clubhead down at the ball put a snap into my downswing. Not trying to shift my weight over to the left side prevented me from getting out ahead of the ball and blocking the shot. Once I understood these two concepts of impact, along with others that will be reviewed thoroughly in this book, things started coming together. When I learned that a push force rather than a pulling force should control the movements of the golf club, and that I should swing down and out through the ball so that my impact path was longer, the secrets to hitting the ball hard were no longer a mystery. I understood the swing intellectually and visually, plus I could repeat a good impact position.

I set the scene for the club to make square and solid contact by taking my address with my hands behind the ball. Additionally, when triggering Croker's automatic motion, it's critical that you push one hand against the other, rehearse the hit position by pressing the hands forward into the impact position, and let the clubhead lag behind the hands in the takeaway; à la Ben Hogan style.

I have no doubt that you will find this book fascinating, and that reading it will open doors that will better enable you to see the swing first in your mind, then make the physical motions that match those images more easily than you ever dreamed. Carefully absorb the words in the text, study the photographs and illustrations, and practice Croker's innovative drills for fast improvement. That way, you will never have more fun getting from Point A to Point B.

Good luck in your quest to improve and have fun experiencing Peter Croker's Path to Better Golf.

JOHN ANDRISANI

INTRODUCTION

In 1961, at age eleven, I caddied for my father at Australia's Sandringham Golf Links. I became hooked on the game after watching him and other golfers hit all kinds of shots in a beautiful green setting. A few weeks later, I began caddying at the Royal Melbourne Golf Club, also in my home country of Australia. Right from the start I was curious about what made one hit a good shot. Later that year I started playing and became even more curious about swing technique. The caddy master at Royal Melbourne, Norm Spence, helped me answer one of the questions regarding the mystery of the swing by showing me the importance of a good address or starting position. "How you start has a lot to do with how you finish," he told me.

Years later, when I was sixteen, I watched Australian

David Graham hitting balls at the Cairns Golf Club until sundown. He and fellow pro Graham Marsh wore the practice fairways out on the Queensland Sunshine Circuit in the middle 1960s. It was then that I realized that hard practice was the only true shortcut to becoming good at golf. These two professionals, plus American Ben Hogan and South African Gary Player, became my idols for their diligent work ethic. The problem was, I didn't exactly know what they were practicing.

Someone else who impressed me greatly during my early years and gave me the incentive to improve was Peter Thomson, who won the British Open five times. Thomson was admired for his clear thinking and simplified approach to golf, and after watching him win a fifth British Open championship in 1965, I was determined to improve.

In my search to find the simplest, most efficient way to swing a club and hit shots solidly and accurately, I queried Thomson and other golf professionals. I also gained knowledge from golf instructors, most notably Bob Toski, Charlie Earp, Paul Runyan, and Jackie Burke. Although I learned enough about the swing to become a fine amateur player, and later a pro, I was still frustrated by my inability to feel in control of the club enough of the time. Don't get me wrong, I know that in golf there is no such thing as perfection. However, I wanted to know how to give myself the best chance of hitting good shots more times than not.

To shorten a long story, for years and years I tried to unravel the mystery of the swing. And although at times I felt myself making progress, not until 1992 did I get excited about sort of breaking through to the other side, thanks to my own research and the help of a team of dedicated Australian golf instructors. In this book, I will share with you these findings and the new and exciting discoveries I have since made to help you get on the Path to Better Golf. For now, I will just whet your appetite and prepare you for your journey by revealing one vital secret to swinging proficiently. In my search for the truth about what makes a good technique tick, I discovered that using a pushing action rather than the commonly taught pulling action is the best way to control the movement of the club. A pushing action controlled by the hands requires less effort, puts less stress on the body, is easier to repeat, and thus gives the golfer the best chance of hitting powerfully accurate shots consistently. I proved this by testing this new swing fundamental on thousands and thousands of amateur and professional golfers around the world.

Although the push-action is vital to my teaching method, there are many more swing secrets to be revealed. In this book, I will give you a detailed account of why you should swing my way and will separate fact from fiction regarding the basic movements of the swing. I will show you how—by hitting putts, chips, and pitch shots, in that order—to familiarize yourself with the correct movements of the hands, arms, and torso. I will explain the back and through movements and show you the easiest way to swing from the top (Point A) into impact (Point B), using great players Ben Hogan and Tiger Woods as models. I will teach you how to groove a good swinging action through practicing drills. Finally, I will teach you how to gain control and consistency.

Let this book serve as your guide to improvement. As you proceed, try to understand each movement intellectually and also try to feel each and every setup position and swinging action. That way, if you go off the path, you can find your way back quickly and easily.

All the best in learning how to master the A-to-B Push-Golf swing technique that will lead you onto the Path to Better Golf.

CHAPTER 1

> # Why You Should Play Golf My Way
>
> *The Push-Golf Swing I Teach Is More Natural and Requires Less Practice Hours to Perfect*

Golf has been played for nearly six hundred years, and during that time there have been great advances in technology. Yet, sadly, a high percentage of recreational players are still shooting the same high scores that they did long ago on the links of St. Andrews in Scotland, the home of golf. Considering that over the last two decades teachers have taken great strides in finding better ways to analyze the swing by computer to pinpoint faults, it is even more surprising that so many enthusiasts play the game so poorly. Even a myriad of special swing gadgets designed to help players improve technique have failed.

One of the reasons you have probably not lowered your handicap all that much is that you have been overloaded with instructional information taught to you by friends or professionals, or that you have read about in golf magazines and books. Frankly, if you were to visit a dozen teachers across the country, asking each to offer a remedy for your slice or to give you a tip that would allow you to hit the ball farther, you would get twelve different answers. The bottom line: there is no set instructional standard that PGA pros follow, and for that reason it is no wonder that you and millions of other golfers are confused. That's the bad news. The good news is that in this book I present my own innovative swing system, one that is not a mix of old methods but something new and fresh, simple to learn, easy to repeat. It is more *natural feeling* and it works. I base this statement on the success I have had teaching players of varying handicaps around the world and watching them hit more fairways and greens and lower their scores in a short time.

Right now, in preparation for the more advanced instruction to come, I will first briefly describe my philosophy. Second, I describe some special aspects of my swing technique, including my balanced, stress-free stance position, the push-action takeaway, the rotor-motor backswing, and the downswing throwing action. This information will provide you with a good base. Further, after employing these positions, I'm sure you will immediately realize how much more natural my teaching system is to learn and repeat over and over.

CROKER'S UNIQUE PHILOSOPHIES: A CRASH COURSE

A Pushing Action Is the Best Path to Better Golf

Pushing the clubhead with the hands, arms, and the body through the ball keeps you in touch with the clubhead and gives you a more powerful and deliberate hit. Think of it as if you are pushing all of the energy out of you, down the clubshaft, and into the ball.

Forget the Smooth-Swing Idea and Make a Tension-Free Aggressive Hit

Boxers, baseball players, and hockey players are all hitters. There is absolutely nothing swinglike about their forward motions. Get in the way of their gloves, bats, hockey sticks, and you'll see how aggressively they hit at their targets: an opponent's jaw, a baseball, a hockey puck.

Golf is a hitting game too. You hit the ball. If for some reason you shift your attention from deliberately hitting the ball and instead try to let some technique do it for you, the game of golf may elude you forever.

Why, When Setting Up to Hit a Tee Shot, You Should Set Your Hands Behind the Clubhead

This address position keeps your hands and the clubshaft connected to your center of gravity, making for a more fluid takeaway action of the hands, arms, and body that can be simply triggered using a forward press action of the hands.

A Push-Action Is the Link to Bringing the Club Up to Point A

Following a forward press—right hand pushing against left—the left hand pushes the slightly resisting right hand back, approximately twelve inches. This push-action triggers the automatic turning action of the hips and shoulders. During the push, no conscious cocking action is employed. Maintaining the slight pressure of left hand against right hand gradually increases the speed of the backswing. This push-action of the hands serves as a governor, encouraging a compact swing, while still creating a full body turn and cocking of the wrists through the momentum of the swinging motion.

Why an Early Hit Is Better Than a Late Hit

You will generate more clubhead speed, and the club will actually stay on the correct path more easily, if you allow your body to be a base while you actively throw the clubhead at the ball the moment you reach the top of the backswing. Simply think of swinging from Point A, the top, to Point B, impact, and compress the ball.

Think of a Hammering Action to Help You Hit the Ball More Solidly

Pound a nail with a hammer as hard as you can. The harder you hit the nail with the hammer—trying without tension to get the hammerhead onto the back of the nail—the greater the angle and the more it is retained between the hammer's shaft and your arm. In short, any late-hit angle is simply the effect of trying to get rid of the late-hit angle. The faster you get rid of the hammer—or the club—the more solid the hit.

Practice This Drill to Feel the Pushing Action

To feel the swing as a pushing action, set up with the club-head against a wall. Push the clubhead against the wall and feel how this pushing is out from and against each of these body parts: head, left shoulder, right shoulder, left hip, right hip, left knee, right knee, left foot, right foot. Now take some practice swings, pushing the clubhead through the ball and away from your entire body. Acquire this feel for all future golf shots.

Reduce Stress on Your Back by Swinging My Way

If your lower body is oriented toward pulling the club, your spine gets caught in the middle with severe twisting and unnecessary pressures.

A pushing orientation does not depend upon the lower body driving forward against the upper body. Pushing is against the entire body and a straight spine. This method is designed to reduce stress on your spine. Actually, many golfers who are unable to play golf anymore because of back and shoulder injuries will be able to play again with this method.

I will go into more detailed differences between the elements of the setup and swing taught by me and the traditional methods taught by others later on in this book. But, again, I first want to provide you with a solid foundation of knowledge step-by-step, so, by the time I present the more complex elements of the swing, you will have no trouble physically repeating the basic movements.

MY METHODS VERSUS TRADITIONAL METHODS
Address

Standing Charlie Chaplin style, with both feet turned outward, allows the hips to turn freely on the backswing and downswing.

In teaching students the setup, I have them stand with both of their feet and knees turned outward. This starting position is better than the traditional one that calls for the left foot to be turned out twenty degrees, the right foot perpendicular to the target line, and both knees turned inward with weight favoring the inside of the feet. My Charlie Chaplin type of setup position allows the hips to turn freely and fully in both directions without putting strain on the knees. Conversely, the traditional golf setup restricts the turn and thus drains power from the swing, plus strains your joints.

Another reason my method of playing is better is that I teach my students to bend from the hips with the butt tucked under and the pelvis tilted up. Based on reactions from my students, this position is much more comfortable than that which is commonly taught: bend from the knees, stick the butt out, keep the pelvis down. More importantly, students who set up my way make a smoother transition into the backswing than those taught the common way, plus tend to keep their hips level rather than tilting them in an exaggerated fashion as most high-handicap players do.

It is a common theory among teachers that it is easier to hit short irons from an *open* stance. They claim that, when you stand open with the feet pointing slightly left of target, it is easier to see the line of the shot and have the hips clear or turn left in the impact area.

You will have much more success playing short irons and long clubs from a *square* stance with the feet parallel to the target line. Based on my work with students of varying handicaps, players feel more confident about aligning themselves to the target and making a fluid hip turn when they start from a square setup position. They have learned from experience that starting from an

Setting up with the feet parallel to the target line, in a "square" position, makes you more confident about hitting the ball squarely and toward the target.

open stance disorients them and makes them slide their hips through impact and hit a *block*, which is a shot that flies right of target.

Backswing

It's better to use a pushing *action rather than a pulling action to propel the club back.*

My system calls for a pushing action on the backswing rather than a pulling action. This may shock you, I know, but not after you realize that a horse does not pull a cart. The horse pushes against the harness as well as against the ground to move the cart. There is a difference as you can see. You just have to look a little deeper to see this true action. The same is true of the golf swing. In short, a pushing action is much more fluid, natural, and powerful than a pulling action.

When you push the right hand against the left to trigger the forward press, then push the left hand back against the right as you swing farther back, you set yourself in position to return the club squarely to the ball at impact. Why? The club swings back on the correct path and plane and stays in front of the body. On the other hand, when you pull on the club with the hands, the tendency is to swing it much too far inside the target line, on a flat path and plane. From this position, even if you have super feel in your hands, are very coordinated, and possess great hand-eye coordination, you will have difficulty returning the clubface to the ball consistently.

Another aspect of the backswing action I recommend involves the turning action of the hips and shoulders. During the turning, the head should be centered to start, then free to rotate as dictated by the swing. I want the turning to be fluid and full, whereas many modern teachers advise students to restrict hip action and keep the head perfectly still while turning the shoulders to the max in an attempt to build torque between the upper and the lower body. Their argument: the greater the tension, the greater the power. I disagree with this theory, largely because trying to restrict the natural turning

Even when playing a short iron my swing technique calls for a free shoulder and hip turn created by a pushing action.

Notice how the hands and clubshaft positions change when moving from the address (top) to the forward press (bottom).

action of the body can lead to serious back injury. Additionally, golfers who strive for a strong shoulder turn and a weak hip turn tend to swing the club back too far to the inside on the takeaway or lift it straight up in the air. Either of these two swing faults causes an off-center hit at impact and an off-line shot.

My rotor-motor backswing is built on the belief that the golfer will attain the best results by maximizing hip turn against the resistance of the knees and feet. In following these directions, you do not have to worry about turning the shoulders, since they will coil automatically as the hips turn. It is thus much more important to turn your hips against your feet than it is to turn your shoulders against your hips. The simple reason for this is that your feet are planted on the ground, giving you a stable base to wind up against. Your hips need to wind against the feet to create a solid foundation for the hands, arms, shoulders, and club to load against.

I also call for lively hands, because I believe positive hand action promotes feel. When you depend on feel, you are more likely to repeat a good swing and put your action back on track fast should you experience a bad patch. The hands turn on or trigger—what I call the rotor-motor in the hips. By employing the correct pushing action of the hands, your hips will turn as if in a barrel, which is what the great teacher Percy Boomer recommended long ago. Let me explain:

The push of the right hand against the left creates the *forward press*—a forward movement of the hands and the club's handle before the swing starts. And when the left hand pushes against the right, it is like turning on the key to an engine. When the hands initiate the swinging action, the hips turn fully and freely forty-five-plus degrees, with the clubhead accelerating as it swings back to the top. At this early stage of the backswing, the slinging action of the clubhead forces the shoulders to turn approximately ninety degrees without you thinking about trying to coil them while restricting hip turn. Furthermore, centrifugal force that is created causes the correct rotation of the clubface and requires no mechanical manipulation. In fact, a natural and automatic "loading" of the club, hands, arms, shoulders, hips, knees, and feet creates a powerful on-path backswing.

I do not understand why so many teachers advise students to keep the hands quiet on the backswing. After all, it is the energy first created by the hands, then the hips, that forces the shoulders to turn and the club to be swung back perfectly on plane. This is why I like to see the left hand cock upward early on, with the thumb pointing upward and the wrists hinging freely and comfortably.

The rotor-motor backswing is a freewheeling tension-free motion, so you are far less likely to hurt your back. Further, timing becomes less important when you are swinging around the central hinge of your hips.

Downswing

For as long as I can remember, golf teachers have been telling students to pull the butt end of the club downward at the start of the downswing while delaying the unhinging action of the wrists.

All power hitters, such as Tiger Woods, create an extreme angle between the clubshaft and left arm in the downswing, and it is only at the last moment that the clubshaft angle releases to accelerate the clubhead into the ball. The fact is, it is not natural or helpful to use a pulling action to accomplish the "delayed hit" as the majority of teachers recommend to students. Because of the feeling of a pull on the left side by

The downswing action: start-down position under way (top) and impact (bottom).

the lagging clubhead, golfers have been tricked into believing the pull concept. This has been the illusion that has stopped golfers from just simply hitting the ball. Once this illusion has been identified and you understand that the pushing action in golf causes the clubhead to move away from its center of rotation, later, and with added acceleration, you are no longer deceived into focusing your attention on the incorrect way to hit the golf ball.

To more easily employ the late-hit action, simply throw the clubhead down at the ball from the top of the backswing like Tiger does. This throwing action triggers the hips, legs, shoulders, and arms to assist the hands in accelerating the club aggressively into the ball at impact.

The secret to the downswing as I see it is getting rid of the clubhead as fast as possible in the direction of the ball. I say this knowing that the effective mass of the clubhead will increase as you increase the thrust and acceleration of the clubhead. Make no mistake, throwing the club at the ball promotes higher clubhead speed and a more powerful shot.

The hands pushing against the grip move the clubhead downward through the ball and cause the body to uncoil powerfully. Pushing the club is much easier to control and makes golf a heck of a lot simpler.

To familiarize yourself with the throwing action, and to feel the down-and-out direction of hit when swinging, practice the following:

1. Address the ball without a club in your hand, letting your arms hang down naturally at your sides.

2. Swing your right arm freely to the top, as shown in the photograph below.

Practice swinging your right arm freely to the top.

3. Throw your hand at the golf ball on the ground, allowing the fingers of your right hand and your right arm to extend in the direction of the ball, as shown in the photograph below.

"Throw" your hand at the golf ball.

Shape of Shot

My method of swinging will allow you to contact the ball squarely and hit straight shots—not fades or draws.

Something else that sets my method apart is that I teach students to hit straight shots instead of selling the fade. The idea that it is much easier to control a fade comes from teachers who believe in a pulling action. When you start the downswing with a pulling action, it is difficult to govern the rate of the clubface closing as it accelerates and releases. Nine out of ten times the clubface will come into impact open rather than square.

When you let a pushing action control the downswing, it is easier to swing the club squarely into the ball. The more you release the clubhead, the straighter the ball will travel.

Perfect Order

Unlike some methods that call for the student to jump right into the mechanics for the full swing, I have the student start with a putt, then progress to a chip, and finally a pitch. Putting teaches you how to develop essentially the very same hand and arm action you will use in the full swing and provides you with a feel of the club-to-ball hit. Chipping teaches you how to coordinate body turn with hand-arm action. Pitching teaches you the art of throwing the club at the ball at a speed closer to that used in the full swing.

Putting: The object of putting is to hit the ball on the correct line at the correct speed. The fewer the moving parts in the stroke, the more solidly and accurately you will hit putts. An efficient putting stroke promotes good feel and good distance control.

I believe that you should use a hands-and-arms motion with minimum shoulder participation to putt, and that the body should stay in a balanced, stable position during the stroke. Let the hands be your major source of the pushing motion in the putting stroke and you will more quickly learn how to best make bigger swings with the longer clubs in your golf bag. What follows are a few tips to give you a head start to learning the golf swing through putting.

Matching this setup position popularized years ago by Billy Casper, one of the game's legendary putters, will help you make a good putting stroke.

Setup Tips: Take a grip with the hands holding the putter predominantly in the fingers with light pressure to promote better feel for the putter's head. Relax both arms and bend them slightly at the elbows and keep both wrists slightly to the sides of the grip. Set your feet parallel to the target line. Bend over from the hips, flex the knees slightly, and set the right shoulder lower than the left. Also, stand with your left leg vertical, your right leg on a slight incline. Set your eyes slightly behind the ball and directly over the target line. Play the ball just inside the front foot.

In swinging the putter back, you should push your left hand against your resisting right hand, just as in the long swing.

Backswing Tips: To start the backswing, tap the putter on the ground lightly several times. This puts you in touch with the putterhead and connects your hands to the motion. Next, employ a slight forward press. Then, push your left hand straight back against a slightly resisting right hand. The right-hand resistance helps control the length of the backswing. This same push-and-resist action is one you will need when swinging other clubs, so practice until you groove it.

Pushing the putter through Jack Nicklaus style, so the left wrist uncocks from its previously level and bent position on the backswing, helps you accelerate the putter into the ball.

Downswing Tips: On the downswing, let both hands move into a fully uncocked condition so that the left wrist straightens, the clubshaft moves in line with the left arm, and the putter's face finishes dead square to the ball. It's this uncocking action that accelerates the putter into and then through the ball. Correct use of the hands (with the shoulders as a base) will give you a much more controlled hit on the ball.

When chipping, it's critical that you employ a forward press action to trigger fluid hip movement and a smooth overall swing.

Chipping: The chip shot is usually played from the fringe of the green with a five, six, seven, or eight iron, with the ball flying a minimal distance in the air before it lands on the green and rolls to the hole like a putt. The mechanics of the chip include controlled body rotation in the backswing and a full uncocking of the wrists down through the ball and into the finish. In my research for the chip and in studying the pros, I was most influenced by the style of Paul Runyan, a two-time winner of the PGA Championship.

Start the backswing by using a forward press with the hands. Let the hands push straight back so the hips turn and the clubhead swings back a short distance.

In making the change of direction, uncock the hands (thumbs down) and push the clubhead down toward the ball. When the ball is struck, the clubhead finishes toe down, toe first. Also, through impact both arms are straight, both wrists are fully uncocked, the clubshaft is in line with the left arm, and the hips have turned fully against the feet.

Once you are convinced that the aforesaid mechanics flow together into one continuous rhythmic motion, from start to finish, work on the thrust level that must be applied to the club through the hands for hitting different-length shots with different clubs. Additionally, work on your routine.

Swing at different speeds when practicing chipping to find your ideal tempo—one that produces shots that fly accurately up to the hole.

Develop a routine that includes a continuous motion of the clubhead, adds rhythm to the chip swing, and assists you in controlling the overall pace of the action. In preparing to swing, use a shortened version of the waggle. Simply rest the clubhead lightly on the ground, then use a wrist-and-hand hinging action to lift it slightly off the turf. Repeat this "tap-lift" action about three times as it will allow you to pre-program the proper hit action. A consistent routine also helps your touch when hitting delicate chip shots.

Pitching: The pitch shot travels farther in air than on the ground. It is mostly played with a pitching wedge, sand iron, or lob wedge.

The mechanics of the pitch are similar to those used in the full swing. You need to hinge the wrist on the backswing and also employ a fluid arm swing and body turn, but just less of it. Also, to ensure solid, square hits, you must let the clubhead

Pitching: the backswing.

Pitching: the throw.

Pitching: the hit.

start back last on the backswing, then throw the clubhead at the ball first on the downswing.

Since the pitch is just a small version of the full swing, and you are new to my method of teaching, study the photographs on pages 24 and 25 showing me hitting a pitch shot to get a feel for the backswing and downward hit.

As you learn gradually, enjoy each step first and concentrate on feeling the motion. Only then will you make a smooth transition into the full swing motion.

Learning in steps is better because it gives you time to absorb the individual motions intellectually, then groove them into one flowing motion through practicing the drills I present in chapter 5. I think you can appreciate that by learning in the order I prescribe, you will remain clearheaded and not arrive on the practice tee or course confused. Moreover, by learning my way you will be more apt to play by feel and repeat a technically sound swinging action.

Golf is not a natural game. It only becomes natural after you understand the fundamentals that fit with your body's most natural movements and have drilled them in. This is why I am against starting a student out in twelfth grade, so to speak. In learning golf my way, you should have the viewpoint of a child starting school and working through the grades. What's most important is first building the framework by understanding the following concepts.

CONCEPT ONE: THE GOLF SWING IS A SWING AND A HIT

Teachers seem to be reviving today the question of whether a player is a hitter or a swinger. Amateurs who hear

The speed of the moving club increases as I move through the hit zone, yet the action feels effortless due to good mechanics.

about this immediately want to categorize themselves. Consequently, players wanting to be swingers swing so slowly that they decelerate the club in the impact zone, and players wanting to be hitters hit so hard they lose control of the club.

I stress the importance of combining a swing action with a hit action, although my system places a bigger emphasis on the all-important hit. That way you will be more likely to swing the club in good tempo and rhythm and nicely time the entire backswing. You need to blend the effortless power of this backswing motion with the direct force of a hitting action on the downswing. To understand this, picture a child on a playground swing. At the start, the swing is directed by a gentle pushing action, just as my golf swing is, then it picks up speed just like the swinging club does. However, the entire to-and-fro action of the swing in the playground is smooth and well timed. By the same token, in the golf swing I help students swing the club back and through smoothly, so it stays on plane in front of the body yet accelerates more and more as the club enters the hit zone near Point B. When you employ such a swing, the most powerful action of throwing the club down at the ball much like you would a sledgehammer at a boulder feels effortless. That effortless feeling is a sign of a technically sound, well-timed action.

CONCEPT TWO: GOLF IS A TWO-TARGET GAME

From experience I have learned that it is better to treat golf as a two-target game than a one-target game. I have

I teach players to hit two targets: the ball and a golf course target, in this case an area of fairway rather than the hole.

found that my students hit many more powerfully accurate shots when ignoring the common tenet to merely swing through toward the ball's target and let the ball "get in the way of a good swing." I believe you will also play better golf if you play according to the two-target approach. Forget the flag. Hit the ball, your first target, solidly and the ball will find your second target, the hole.

Target One—the Ball: You will give yourself the best possible chance of hitting your first target—the ball—solidly and squarely if you set the club down correctly. To achieve this goal, the bottom or sole of the club must be virtually flush to the turf. Also, the center of the clubface must be behind the back center portion of the ball or just a little toe-side of center. You must also appreciate that in the hitting area the club must swing down, out, then through the ball.

Target Two—the Hole (or area of fairway or green): Logically, the ball needs a target, since the main aim of golf is to take the least number of shots to hit the ball into the hole. You will give yourself the best chance of swinging the club on the correct path and plane and hitting the ball up and forward toward the target by (1) setting the clubface perpendicular to the target, whether that's a hole or an area of the green or fairway—and (2) aligning your feet, knees, hips, and shoulders parallel or *square* to an imaginary line running from the ball to the target—the *target line*.

CONCEPT THREE: IMAGERY WILL HELP YOU MAKE A TENSION-FREE SWING

Another reason you should learn to play my way is because I provide you with specific images or visual aids to

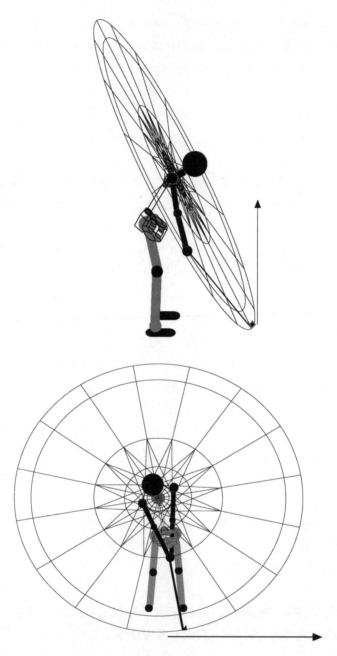

Imagining the swing as a wheel takes your mind off technique and, as a result, boosts your confidence.

quickly put you on the Path to Better Golf. By viewing the swing as a wheel with an axle, motor, and key, you will be more likely to be comfortable with the complete action and not become intimidated over the ball when you are preparing to hit a shot.

To appreciate the use of imagery, examine the illustration opposite. Think of the clubhead as being on the rim of a wheel. See the clubshaft and the arms as spokes in the wheel. See the hub or center of the wheel located at the base of the neck. Imagine the spine acting as the axle. Imagine the hips as the rotor-motor, mounted on the legs as a foundation. The knees are shock absorbers, and the ankles pivot points. The hands are the key to this powerful engine. They are what turn the motor on.

Through pushing with the hands, the hips (rotor-motor) rotate back and through. The hips turn the spine (axle). The axle spins the spokes (arms and clubshaft). In turn, the club-head swings as if on the rim of the wheel.

Take this image to the practice tee or the course and I guarantee you will be much more clear-minded and less apt to freeze over the ball because you have so many swing thoughts swimming around in your head. Just turn on the ignition to make a free-flowing swing, one that allows you to hit your first target—the ball—and hit your second target—the hole.

CONCEPT FOUR: THE SMART GOLFER COPIES A SUCCESSFUL PRO

What helped me improve was choosing one golfer of similar height, weight, and body type to model myself after. Don't get me wrong, in refining my swing theory I have learned directly from many great professionals, including Peter Thomson, Gary Player, David Graham, Norman Von Nida, Lee Trevino, Sam Snead, Seve Ballesteros, and Vijay Singh. However, as a model I chose Ben Hogan because he's built like me—average height, average weight, and strong muscle stroke. Plus, like me, Hogan emphasized body rotation.

I encourage my students to learn the Push-Golf fundamentals I have been refining since 1992. However, I am not a pure method teacher because I also encourage players to understand the various nuances of the swinging action by seeing how other players built like them get the job done. I also want you to watch the pros on television or live at a tournament and take notes on exactly what someone like you does to hit the ball solidly and accurately. Next, try to incorporate some of their movements of the swing into the framework I provide you with.

Making golf simple to master can only be achieved by knowing the fundamentals, drilling in the fundamentals, and finally letting go of these fundamentals and experimenting on your own with such subjective elements of the swing as grip pressure and tempo.

If in your quest to improve you get stuck, you have probably misunderstood a concept, not totally grooved a particular swing action correctly, missed a step in the total motion, or let your conscious mind interfere with the subconscious reflex swing movements you have developed in practice. Simplicity by omission does not make something simple, only incomplete and ineffective. For this reason, go through all of the stages of learning slowly enough to absorb all of what I teach you, then move on to create your own personal swing keys either by observing a pro model or through experimentation in practice. The rewards will be a controlled golf swing of effortless power, a freewheeling motion of the club around a steady center, coupled with an increased confidence in your ability to play this wonderful game.

CONCEPT FIVE: PRACTICE MAKES YOU THINK LESS AND FEEL MORE

I am very big on playing by feel and essentially letting the swing operate on automatic pilot, rather than through consciously directing the movement of the club on the backswing and downswing.

It's healthy to think about shot-making strategies on the course, but not about the golf swing. So many high-handicap players try to think their way from the address to the backswing to the downswing, as if connecting dots. Good golfers do not do this. They let the swing flow, based on the mechanics they work hard to groove in practice through drill-work.

As you learn golf my way, I encourage you to practice the push-swing action over and over so that you feel and ingrain the proper actions. Only after you drill this action in can you play by feel and enjoy the hit.

I even relate the short game to the full swing. As I said earlier, I first have students putt, chip, and pitch to help them learn the complexities of the swinging action in a simple way—through drill-work. For example, here's a chipping drill I use to help students familiarize themselves with the various movements in the real swing.

Step One: Take your address position, with the feet close together and 70 percent of your body weight on the left foot.

Hold a yardstick so approximately six inches of the stick protrudes past the heel pad of the left hand. Place the right-hand fingertips against the side of the yardstick.

Step Two: Push the right hand forward against a slightly resisting left hand. Note the slight hip turn to the left—the "forward press."

Step Three: Push the wrist area of the left hand back against the slightly resisting right-hand fingers. When the handle end starts to move back in advance of the bottom end of the yardstick, note how the hip turn leads and, in turn, moves the shoulders, hands, arms, and yardstick back. Note too how the end of the yardstick continues to point at the target line.

Step Four: When the hands reach a spot opposite the right foot, uncock the wrists so that the yardstick moves fully in line with the left arm. Now note where the yardstick points.

Step Five: Push the right hand against the left hand so the end of the yardstick moves directly toward the ball. Resist with the left hand and you will feel the left hip turn naturally, the left leg straighten, the shoulders square up to the target, and the right arm move from a slightly bent position to a straight position as the hips turn.

Step Six: As the right arm straightens, the hands release the yardstick through the ball while it remains in line with the left arm.

Step Seven: Once you have learned to educate your hands, plus rehearsed the vital steps of chipping, hit shots with an eight iron, using the same swing keys you just learned, but swing at a brisker pace. Note how far the ball flies in the air and how far it rolls when you swing at different speeds. Repeat this drill to learn to coordinate hip and hand action.

When practicing the Yardstick Drill, it's critical that the yard-stick and the left arm line up during the backswing (left) and downswing (right).

Movement #1

Thinking of swinging the club back to Point A, then down to Point B, encourages you to make an efficient motion and hit the ball powerfully with minimal effort.

When a throwing motion of the hands is used to trigger the downswing, the body practically becomes electrified and plays a strong supporting role in accelerating the club into the golf ball.

Movement #3

Imagining that the ball is a rock and you want to crush it using a powerful "throwing" motion raises your level of confidence and allows you to hit the ball consistently to your target.

Movement #4

Pushing the club into the ball at impact, with the left arm and clubshaft virtually in a straight line, helps you add torque to the shaft and power to the shot.

Movement #5

At Point A, when the club reaches the top, the right wrist should be bent back slightly just like Ben Hogan's is here, and the shoulders should have turned more than the hips.

Movement #6

As Hogan proves here, the downswing hip turn starts while the backswing is still in progress. Copy Hogan and you will be better poised to throw the club down into the ball.

Movement #7

To generate high clubhead speed on the downswing, use your hands to flail the clubhead toward the ball as fast as possible while maintaining a smooth rhythm—Hogan style.

Movement #8

A balanced finish indicates that you pushed the club correctly down from Point A to Point B, and swung through all the right positions as easily as a child connects dots on a page.

When you push the club back to the top like Tiger Woods, your hips should turn, as if in a barrel, forty-five degrees and your shoulders about ninety degrees.

If you make hitting the ball your number-one priority, à la Woods, you will be more apt to accelerate the hands and club powerfully on the downswing and hit long shots.

To ensure solid contact, Woods lets the body turn through the shot automatically as a result of the throw, rather than consciously clearing the hips and shoulders.

In hitting through to Point B, let your right arm extend, your right knee move in toward your left knee, and your shoulders unwind—just like Tiger.

CHAPTER 2

> # False-Data Stripping
>
> *The First Step to Playing Good*
> *Golf Is to Determine What's*
> *Wrong and What's Right About*
> *Common Swing Tips*

I like my students to think of the golf swing as one uninter-rupted flowing motion. I also teach students to examine the flight of the ball to determine how well they are doing. If the shot flies on target, the tempo, rhythm, and timing of their swing must have been good. Also, good shots and a flowing motion only come when there is no blockage in the brain. Blockage usually comes in the form of conscious swing thoughts that a player has learned through an instructor, a book, or a magazine article. I'm not suggesting that all swing thoughts are bad. Even top pros use a single swing thought to promote a good swinging action, but here's the difference. Through practice, they *know* that this swing thought works for them, just as I know that mine works for me. You too can find value in reviewing a single swing thought, such as *Thumbs down through impact*. Having said that, if you clog your brain with numerous swing thoughts, or one wrong one, you will probably not swing well and hit on-target shots.

In teaching adult men and women, junior players, and seniors, I have witnessed players hit off-line shots because they swung the club while thinking about something they should not have been thinking about. I am talking here about common tips, false advice presented as fact, such as "Shift your weight to the right foot on the backswing," "Create a wide swing arc on the backswing," and "Pull the club's handle down with your left hand to trigger the downswing." So you don't run into the same traps, let me review the most common tips and set you straight about what's wrong and what's right so you'll be put back on the Path to Better Golf.

In the early stage of the swing, the left hand should push while the right hand resists.

Common Swing Tip #1: Pull the club back with the right hand.

What's Wrong: Starting the backswing by pulling on the club's handle with the right hand causes the player to swing too fast, with the clubhead usually moving too far inside the target line or straight up in the air. When you swing on an overly flat plane, it is difficult to redirect the club to a square impact position. When you pick the club up on a steep path, you prevent the right hip from freely turning back and the swing's rotor-motor from generating power.

What's Right: *You should push the left hand against a slightly resisting right hand to trigger the backswing.*

Let the clubhead trace a natural arc and the clubface open slightly in the takeaway as the body turns.

Common Swing Tip #2: Swing the club straight back along the target line.

What's Wrong: Concentrating on swinging the club straight back causes the clubface to shut or point downward on the backswing. As a result, the shoulders turn on too steep a plane and the hips sway instead of turning.

What's Right: *Pushing the left hand against the right hand to start the swing causes the clubhead to trace a natural arc as the hip turn slings the clubhead back and up. So let the club swing open slightly on the backswing as the body turns, just as Hogan did.*

The classic fault of turning the shoulders to start the backswing makes you move the club on too flat a plane.

Common Swing Tip #3: Turn your left shoulder in a clockwise direction to trigger the backswing.

What's Wrong: By consciously trying to use the big muscles in the left shoulder to trigger the backswing, you run the risk of the clubhead path moving too far inside the target line once your hip turn comes into play. The sequence of shoulders then hips requires additional hand and arm manipulation to stop the natural tendency to swing top flat.

What's Right: *Use your hands to trigger the hip turn before turning your shoulders. That way, you will keep the club in front of the body on the backswing and be poised to deliver the clubface squarely to the ball.*

Another common fault of the high-handicap player is trying so hard to swing the club back in one piece that the arms tense up. See the tension in the arms. This backswing fault causes you to lose clubhead feel and power.

Common Swing Tip #4: Employ a one-piece takeaway of the arms, hands, and club.

What's Wrong: Trying to swing back in one piece with the wrists locked makes you wooden due to tension created in the arms, and hands. As a result, you lose feel for the swinging clubhead and end up hitting an off-line shot.

What's Right: *Let the forward press action of the right hand against the left initiate the correct hip action, then let the backward takeaway motion of the hands turn the hips, rotate the shoulders, and sling the arms, hands, and club away from the ball.*

This is what you call natural wrist action created by the momentum of the swinging clubhead.

Common Swing Tip #5: Cock your wrists in the backswing.

What's Wrong: Consciously trying to cock your wrists in the backswing can cause an overly long and loose swinging action.

What's Right: *Let the momentum of the swinging clubhead cause the left wrist to cock and right wrist to bend as the clubhead accelerates past the body into the backswing.*

On the backswing, I want a student to feel pressure in the left heel, left thigh, and left hip as a counterbalance to the clubhead swinging back.

Common Swing Tip #6: Shift your weight to your right foot on the backswing.

What's Wrong: Never consciously try to shift your weight to your right foot on the backswing, since this will likely cause the body to sway. In turn, you will lose your balance and hit a bad shot.

What's Right: *In the backswing, the hands, arms, and club move dynamically to the right, with their effective mass off-center to the backside. This weight transfer needs to be counterbalanced by the hip-turning action. So when swinging back, with the hips turning freely, as if in a barrel, you should feel pressure build in the left heel, left knee, left thigh, and hip.*

It's critical that instead of consciously turning the left shoulder, you let hand action trigger this vital backswing movement.

Common Swing Tip #7: Turn your left shoulder under your chin on the backswing.

What's Wrong: Golfers who follow these instructions tend to tilt the head toward the shoulder and reverse pivot—set too much weight on their left side. This faulty position will cause problems of balance on the downswing and misdirection of the clubhead in the hitting area.

What's Right: *The best players in the world let the left shoulder turn automatically. The takeaway action of the hands causes the hips to rotate and the clubhead to swing back and up. Next, the shoulders coil naturally.*

On the backswing, the left knee should rotate outward, not inward.

Common Swing Tip #8: Rotate the left knee behind the ball.

What's Wrong: In an effort to encourage the student to turn behind the ball and shift weight to the right foot, many teachers advise students to rotate their left knee behind the ball.

Golfers who try this turn the knee inward so much that they encourage the right hip to overturn. Consequently, they end up swinging as in a teacup—on an exaggerated flat plane. This fault makes it difficult to square the clubface to the ball at impact and hit an accurate shot.

What's Right: *The left knee must move more outward. This will give you a much stronger windup from the hips down. Also, if the knee moves correctly, it will be poised to straighten correctly on the downswing and cause the left hip to turn faster. As a result, a passageway will open up for you to freely hit the ball.*

Common Swing Tip #9: Create a wide swing arc on the backswing.

What's Wrong: Students are often told to swing the hands well past the body, with the wrists locked, to create a wide arc of swing and generate power. Ironically, if you heed this advice, you will disconnect the arm swing from the body turn and lose power.

What's Right: *The loading of the backswing by the swinging clubhead puts you into a coiled position, with the hips and shoulders wound up, and the hands and arms readied for the throw. This windup, together with a free and natural wrist-cock, helps create power. In turn, the throwing action of the clubhead on the downswing releases this power and sends powerful energy into the ball.*

Common Swing Tip #10: Restrict hip turn on the backswing.

What's Wrong: One school of thought among today's teachers is that to create power in the golf swing the player should wind the shoulders and upper torso against the hips and legs. If you follow this advice, hip turn is restricted and the turning shoulders start the backswing. This way of turning puts undue strain on the back and tends to cause the clubhead to swing off the proper path. Also, because the lower body winds up last, balance is difficult to maintain.

What's Right: *I call for the hips to wind freely against the knees and feet, which I believe creates power and a solid base to swing from.*

Common Swing Tip #11: Keep the left arm stiff during the backswing.

What's Wrong: Following this advice will create tension in the arm that will ultimately disrupt the throwing on the downswing and cause the club to decelerate in the impact area.

What's Right: *The correct pushing action of your hands will keep your left arm extended, but in a relaxed manner, giving you good structure both in the backswing and the downswing.*

Common Swing Tip #12: Pull the club's handle down with your left hand to trigger the downswing.

What's Wrong: The number one illusion in golf is that, in the transition from the backswing to the downswing, the golfer pulls the club down into the back of the ball. This seems especially true if you look at slow-motion, stop-action film of the swing. The golfer swinging does sense a pull on the muscles, particularly those in the left arm and shoulder, but it's really the push against the clubhead at the change of direction that causes this sensation.

This powerful downswing action into the ball is created by a pushing motion of the hands and does not depend on leg thrust.

Because some instructors are fooled into believing that the downswing is controlled by a pulling action, their students pull the club down with the left hand. This fault usually causes the golfer to swing from outside to inside the target line and hit a pull slice or slide forward and block the ball out to the right.

What's Right: *Throwing a ball seems like it is a pulling action too. But any top major league pitcher will tell you it's a pushing motion. So once your reach the top of the backswing, push (throw) the club into the ball with your hands.*

Common Swing Tip #13: Drive the legs toward the target on the downswing.

What's Wrong: During the 1960s and 1970s, when Jack Nicklaus was frequently winning golf tournaments, the editors of a popular golf magazine concluded that he generated power by driving the legs toward the target. Consequently, numerous articles were written about Nicklaus's leg drive. Golfers, believing this would help them hit the ball longer, started trying to copy Nicklaus. The problem was they mistook a lateral shift of the lower body for an aggressive lunge. As a result, they got well out in front of the ball, with their lower body outrunning their hands and arms. When the lower body slides, the clubface doesn't have time to square up. At impact, the clubface is open and the shot flies right of target.

What's Right: *In the downswing, it is the hands that throw the clubhead at the ball. This action causes the lower body to react accordingly, without your thinking about anything. Additionally, the shoulders tilt and rotate, and the arms swing down to support the hands in delivering the club powerfully on the correct path down to the ball.*

Common Swing Tip #14: Keep your head down and behind the ball.

What's Wrong: If you want to injure your neck and hit a fat shot, follow this common direction to keep the head down and behind the ball until well after impact. I don't know who started giving golfers this advice long ago, but for some reason it stuck. And that is precisely why many students who come to me for lessons find it difficult to accelerate the club in the impact zone and finish the swing without losing their balance.

What's Right: *Let the momentum of the swinging club and the forces exerted on the body at impact bring your head up. The eyes need to be watching the ball so that once the ball has been hit, the head rotates toward the target with the eyes following the ball. This release action of the head allows you to hit through solidly with the body completing its full turning motion to the finish.*

Two top professionals, David Duval of the PGA Tour and Annika Sorenstam of the LPGA Tour, take free head movement to the extreme. They let their head release toward the target before impact. You may want to give this look-see action a try if you have trouble generating a high enough clubhead speed and making a free-feeling downswing action.

Common Swing Tip #15: The impact position should match the address.

What's Wrong: The address position is passive, rather static, while the impact position is active. The only real similarity between the two positions is that the clubface is square to the ball and target. However, if you try to arrive at impact with the hips parallel to the target line, as they were at address, you will cause the clubhead to decelerate and the clubface to finish open to the target.

What's Right: *All you have to do is look at a stop-action photo of any great ball striker to see that impact, compared to address, comprises very different alignments of the body, arms, hands, and wrists. The dynamic motion of the golf swing and the increase in the effective mass of the clubhead cause the body to turn in advance of the clubhead's reaching impact.*

Let the hands swing the club downward so that the hips

*clear to the left of the target line and make room for the club to
swing freely into the ball. If you realize that the downswing only
takes one-fifth second from the top—Point A—to the ball—Point
B—you can appreciate that you don't have time to think about
anything, let alone trying to match the address position.*

Common Swing Tip #16: Keep the right wrist bent at
impact.

What's Wrong: Trying to keep the right wrist hinged at
the moment of impact is crazy, since you will drain power
from the swing and cause the shot to fly off-line.

*As you can see, the impact position shown here is much more
active than the address. Also, the head does not stay behind the
ball and the right wrist does not stay bent as you fully release.*

What's Right: *The correct pushing action of the hands will have the right wrist correctly bent until late in the downswing, yet as you fully uncock both hands through the impact zone, the right wrist will straighten (as will the left), which makes for a solid, square hit.*

Common Swing Tip #17: Hold the clubface square through impact.

What's Wrong: Attempting to consciously hold the clubface square stops its natural rotation in the hitting area. As a result, the clubface points right of target at impact, causing the ball to fly to the right of the target.

What's Right: Ben Hogan Way: *Ben Hogan discovered a way to release the clubface through impact without fearing the hook shot. He releases the clubface from open to closed, but because he does not try to hold the clubface square, it closes naturally and goes along with his hip rotation in the impact area. Follow his example and you too will hit on-target shots.*

Most PGA Tour professionals hit a controlled fade or a gentle draw, so their clubface does not finish square to the target line at impact. The irony is, even if you are intending to hit a straight shot, you should never force the clubface to stay square, particularly just after impact when the club wants to close and rotate to the inside.

Common Swing Tip #18: Rotate the right forearm over the left through impact.

What's Wrong: Many golfers who leave the clubface wide open at impact are given the aforesaid advice by teachers. The fact is, rotating the forearms usually causes the player to flick the club closed and duck-hook the ball as a result.

What's Right: *If you are looking to get rid of a slice, throw the clubhead at the ball with the feeling of letting its toe end lead its heel end. This full throw gives you a constant rate of clubface closure through impact with a minimum of timing needed.*

Common Swing Tip #19: Maintain the spine angle in the finish.

What's Wrong: Following this bit of advice is likely to promote timing problems, off-center hits, and damage to your back.

What's Right: *If you swing down correctly, using a throwing motion, you will never be able to maintain your spine angle. The momentum of the swinging club in the impact area releases the shoulder turn and in turn moves the head and the body up into a balanced finish. Thus, your posture moves to an upright-standing, balanced position.*

CHAPTER 3

Building Blocks

*The Elements of Grip, Stance,
Posture, Alignment, and Aim
Determine the Type of Swing You
Employ and the Shot You Hit*

All golfers seek consistency. They want to hit the ball more accurately into the middle of the fairway or the green, yet go about reaching their goal in the wrong way. The typical club-level player concentrates hard on trying to develop a perfect swing when in fact he or she should first work to build a solid, technically sound address position.

The average PGA Tour professional knows not to put the cart before the horse. Realizing that the address is the engine room of the swing, he works on the elements of grip, stance, posture, alignment, and aim, just as Jack Nicklaus did when he was setting records in the 1960s, 1970s, and 1980s. In fact, Jack Nicklaus, the player with the greatest winning record in golf, said this in his book *Golf My Way:*

"If you set up correctly, there's a good chance you'll hit a reasonable shot, even if you make a mediocre swing. If you set up incorrectly, you'll hit a lousy shot even if you make the greatest swing in the world."

When Nicklaus worked on the setup with his longtime coach, the late Jack Grout, they did not just merely review each component. They tied everything together by developing a set routine, one that Nicklaus still uses today. Even though the routines of professional golfers vary, they are similar in many ways. It's worth taking a look at what Nicklaus has done so well for his entire career in preparing for a shot.

Nicklaus starts his routine from a point directly behind the ball. He stares with intense concentration down the fairway. First, he picks the target, the ball's landing area, then he selects a mark on the ground a few feet ahead of him directly on the target line as his close-up aiming point. Next, he programs himself to make the correct swing by running a mental movie of the ball flying on the line and along the trajectory he has so carefully chosen. Next, he carefully steps into the shot, always with the right foot easing into place first, and sets the clubhead behind the ball with its face aligned precisely for the type and degree of side spin he intends to give the shot. Then, carefully looking back and forth from the ball to his interim target, he eases the club and his body into their final positions. Next, he raises the clubhead slightly above the ground, waggles it lightly a time or two, then sets the center of the face almost flush to the back of the ball and slightly above the ground. Finally, he's ready to start the swing.

As legendary Spanish player Seve Ballesteros once said about Nicklaus's routine:

"The way he works his body into the setup and builds a balanced foundation from the feet upward is really a beautiful sight. His entire preswing process flows as smoothly and cohesively as a piece by Mozart. If you need a model for your own address procedure, you'd have to look long and hard to find a better one."

I agree with Seve, my friend and former student. The setup is one area of the game where you lack an excuse for not matching the same positions as Nicklaus and other pros. Unless you are handicapped in some way, you should be able to assume a technically sound grip, stand to the ball correctly in an athletic position with good posture, set the club's face perpendicular to the ball and the target, and align your body parallel to the target line.

Before walking you through the address routine for a shot, and telling you how the setup flows together, I'd like to first briefly introduce each component.

When the fingers of the left hand wrap around the club's grip, they should touch the palm lightly.

GRIP

A good grip sets up the correct alignments that totally support hitting the ball squarely and solidly at impact. For all to go as planned, and to poise yourself to hit an on-target shot, make sure at the start that the actual grip on the club is the correct size for your hand. When the fingers of the left hand wrap around the grip, they should touch the palm lightly. If this is not the case, see your pro, so he can put the proper-size grip on your club.

In setting up, encourage straight shots by imagining a target line running parallel to a second line across the feet.

STANCE

To promote an on-plane swing and be poised to return the clubface squarely to the ball at impact, an imaginary line across the feet should parallel a second imaginary line running from the ball to the target.

When taking your stance, be sure that the left leg is vertical, the right leg is angled toward the target, and the right shoulder is set lower than the left.

POSTURE

When taking your stance, bend from the ball-and-socket joints of the hips and unlock the knees somewhat so that your spine is comfortably straight. Tilt the pelvis up, since this position reduces strain on the back and encourages the hips to turn freely in a barrel. Set the right shoulder lower than the left. The shoulder and spine tilt allows the left arm to hang down in a comfortably extended position and the right arm to be slightly bent with the right elbow pointing down in front of the right hip. The left leg should be in a vertical position, while the right leg is angled toward the target. The arms should hang down naturally in a relaxed fashion. The longer the club, the higher the hands naturally ride. You should feel heavy in the feet, relaxed from the waist up, and springy from the waist down.

In teaching circles across the country, it is often said that weight should be focused on the inside section of the feet, so that body sway is prevented. I don't agree with this advice at all, for the simple reason that this setup stops the proper coil actions from the ankles to the hips.

I believe that weight should be centrally balanced on both feet, since this allows you to turn freely with no fear of straining the back. The feet should be spread shoulder-width apart for the long clubs, heel-width apart for the shorter clubs. Additionally, both feet should be turned out approximately thirty degrees. Further, both knees should be bent slightly and point out toward the toes. These feet and knee positions allow you to establish a stable base to swing and hit from.

To promote accurate drives, set the clubface and body square to the ball as well as a target area in the fairway.

ALIGNMENT

To promote a rotary, balanced swing and square impact, the feet, knees, hips, and shoulders should be positioned parallel to the target line. Setting the clubface down correctly will ensure good body alignment.

Something else that will affect body alignment is the position of the hands. It is far easier to take the club away on the correct path if the hands are centered or placed opposite the middle of the body, rather than well ahead of the ball.

Start your preswing routine from behind the ball.

AIM

The clubface should be positioned perpendicular to the ball and the target.

THE ADDRESS ROUTINE

To obtain a harmonic swing and hit on-target shots consistently, follow a set preswing routine. During the routine, you will align the hands, arms, and body to the club, and in turn the club to the ball and the ball's target. Sticking to the same routine when preparing to hit shots allows you to develop a smooth tempo and rhythm, with the swing operating essentially on automatic pilot once you take the club away. So let me now explain through words and pictures the various steps of the routine.

Step One: Select the club for the shot at hand, then walk to a position some three to four paces behind the ball, keeping the ball directly between you and the target.

Step Two: Pick an intermediary spot between the ball and the target, approximately one to two yards ahead of the ball and directly on the target line.

Step Three: Let the intermediate target spot you designated serve as an alignment aid as you walk to the side of the ball.

Step Four: In adjusting your grip, make sure that the club's handle is wedged under the heel pad of your left hand. Make sure too that the handle runs diagonally across the left hand from the crease in your palm between your little finger and heel pad to the second knuckle joint of your index finger.

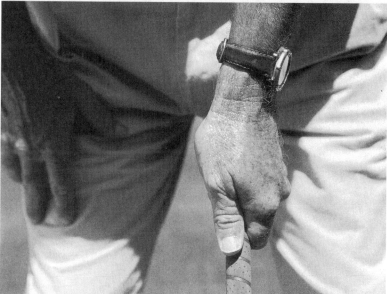

In gripping, make certain that the club's handle lies diagonally across the left hand (left) and is wedged under the heel pad (above top). Be sure too that the left thumb is positioned to the side of the handle (above bottom).

Hold the club predominantly in the fingers of the right hand (top), with the thumb pointing down the left side of the grip (bottom) and the little finger either overlapping the left forefinger (opposite top) or interlocking with it (opposite bottom).

Position the left thumb slightly right of center on the top of the grip, with the V formed by it and the left forefinger pointing up at your right shoulder.

Step Five: Hold the club predominantly in the fingers of the right hand, with the middle two fingers gripping the handle more firmly and the lifeline of your right hand covering your left thumb. Let the little finger of your right hand either overlap the left forefinger or interlock with it. The hollow in your right palm, along the lifeline, should be directly behind your left thumb and fit snugly to the club's handle with no gaps. Let your right thumb sit on the top left-hand side of the grip, so the V formed by your right thumb and forefinger points up at your right shoulder. Check that your right wrist is flat and square to your left wrist, and that both wrists are parallel to the club's leading edge.

Step Six: Hold the club in a vertical position to get a feel for the club and simultaneously stare at the target.

During this push-swing process, the grip should be light and you should get the feeling that you are balancing the club

When standing to the side of the ball and holding the club in a vertical position, stare at the target and start imagining the ball flying toward it.

When lowering the club to a horizontal position, check that its leading edge is vertical to the ground.

in both hands. This "balancing act" allows you to feel the clubhead. Maintain that sensation throughout the swing.

Step Seven: Lower the clubshaft to a horizontal position opposite your belt buckle, making sure that the clubhead's leading edge is vertical to the ground. Next, make sure that as you push down from the left hand's heel and wrist area that your left wrist is positioned on top of the grip and your right wrist is parallel to it. Both hands should feel part of a unit. Now that you have positioned yourself to the clubface, club-

After stepping into the ball with your left foot and jockeying the feet into a square, shoulder-width stance, be sure that you can comfortably lift your toes off the ground, as this ensures central-ized weight distribution.

shaft, and clubhead, you are ready to position yourself to the golf ball.

Step Eight: Starting from a balanced position on your right foot, bend from your hips and lower the club. Next, set your left foot in position, correctly aligned with the ball. Jockey the right foot and body into a square position aligned to the ball's target.

The clubhead's leading edge should be perpendicular to the target. The butt end of the clubshaft should point just below the navel, or at the body's center of gravity, so that when you trigger the swing with a forward press action the hips turn slightly counterclockwise.

During this stage of the address routine, you want to feel that you are standing a comfortable distance from the ball. The consistency of the distance you stand from the ball and of the ball's relation to your feet is critical to hitting the ball squarely and solidly. Proper posture helps you get these things right. However, also be sure that you are able to lift your toes off the ground. That way, the balance between the balls of the feet and the heels is constant. Make sure that the toe end of each foot points outward approximately thirty degrees. Be sure, too, that the ball is played off the left instep or heel for wood shots and a couple of inches back from the left heel for irons.

Step Nine: Rotate or "waggle" the clubhead away and then back down toward the ball about three to five times. The waggle has you hinge your right wrist back, then uncock it down, then return it to a flat or vertical position as you square the club to the intended line of flight.

During the waggle, both hands push against the grip of the club from predominantly the heel-pad and wrist areas. The pushing action of the hands rotates the forearms, stretches the left arm from the shoulder to the wrist, and bends the right elbow forward and in front of the right hip. In the process, the left wrist cocks and the right wrist bends back.

Once the hands are set in the backswing section of the waggle, the wrists uncock down (thumbs down) and allow the clubface to remain facing outward. As the wrists approach a fully uncocked position, the left heel pad pushes back and down while the right thumb and forefinger push against the side of the grip and forward too. These dual pushing actions

Here you see the backswing waggle in two movements.

cause the forearms to rotate and in turn the clubface to square up with the ball and target. The waggle programs the hands, arms, and wrists for the upcoming swing, promotes clubhead feel, and helps create the correct tension level in the muscles.

It's critical that, during the waggle, you keep moving your feet and jockeying yourself into a balanced address position as Tiger Woods does. This preswing procedure helps promote a rhythmic swing. Tiger and other fine players also look up to the target and back to the ball during the waggle since this preswing procedure promotes and confirms good alignment, relaxes them, and raises their confidence level. If you know you are aligned correctly, you will feel better about making a good swing and hitting an accurate shot.

Step Ten: After completing the waggle, give the clubhead a tap, tap, tap on the grass, set the clubhead down lightly on the turf behind the ball, then proceed into the forward press. The purpose of the forward press is primarily to program the body for its upcoming function in the golf swing— namely the smooth transition into the backswing. You employ the forward press by pushing the right hand forward against a slightly resisting left hand. As you proceed with the forward press, the hips turn, particularly the left one. Also the left shoulder rises up while the right shoulder moves down around a steady head. The right elbow bends slightly more as the elbow moves a little forward in front of the body. The left knee straightens slightly. The weight moves through the left heel and toward the right heel, triggering a rounded hip turn.

The forward press function of the swing unlocks the body from a static position, promoting the correct rotation of the hips and the shoulders. Further, it spring-loads the body,

The reason you can see my left trouser pocket from this viewpoint is that I've moved the hands well forward of the ball. This forward press action preturns the hips. In fact, the forward press triggers a number of body movements that resemble those at impact.

arms, and hands. The clubface remains square to the target line but is hooded down ever so slightly. As you employ the forward press, you should feel a slight curling under of the last three fingers of the left hand. As these fingers curl under, the upper left arm is compressed slightly against the upper chest area, giving you a real connected and linked feeling. This forward press is where you discover that golf is more a hands-and-hips game than an arms-and-shoulders game. The added bonus: the forward press gives you a feel for the body positions at impact.

Step Eleven: The takeaway begins. The pressure of the left hand against a slightly resisting right hand starts the backward action. At this point in the swing, knee action is critical to creating a full coil of the body and a balanced rotation of the hips against the feet. The left knee moves outward while the flexed right knee rotates clockwise slightly due to the turning hips. During this segment of the backswing, when the lower body winds up, you should feel as if you are "corkscrewing" down into the ground.

CHAPTER 4

A to B

*An Easy Way to Swing to the Top
(Point A), Then Down to the Ball
(Point B)*

Chances are you have hit a supersolid, superaccurate tee shot at least once in your life and concluded that the sensation of swinging felt effortless. Top tour professionals are familiar with this feeling because they have perfected the mechanical elements of the setup and swing, plus grooved good tempo, timing, and rhythm, all through diligent practice.

You have already learned the vital components of the address and address routine, so you are already far along the Path to Better Golf. However, to stay on that path and learn to consistently hit the ball powerfully and accurately, you must learn the ins and outs of the takeaway; the technical elements in swinging the club up to the top, Point A; the secrets to swinging down to the ball, Point B; and the actions of the follow-through and finish.

SWINGING BACK AND UP TO POINT A

The takeaway action causes the effortless slinging motion of the clubhead. The left hand's function, as it moves straight back for approximately twelve inches, is to cause the shoulders to rotate, the left wrist to bend, and the clubhead to move away last. The slight right-hand resistance promotes the turning of the right hip. While this left- and right-hand action occurs, the active pressure in them causes the hips to fully coil

As the left hand moves straight back early in the takeaway, it triggers a clockwise turning action of the shoulders. From this angle you can also see that the left knee moves outward, another key to a good backswing pivot action.

Hip turn is directly related to hand movement. In the above photograph you can see that the hands only moved a short distance, yet the hips and legs have been wound up against the feet to help launch the clubhead into the backswing.

against the feet. Throughout this early stage of the swing, the arms, hands, and club feel as if they're being left behind the body's pivot action.

Various levels of precision can be attained in this area, and it is important for you to realize that learning the body pivot needs to be done step-by-step if you are going to take your swing to the golf course and be confident. The most simple, basic body-pivot action—left knee out, left knee straight—is where you should start. And you must work to groove this action in practice, because if you try to consciously think about employing it while playing for score, you will hit off-line shots.

The body pivot is the motor of the golf swing. The hands are the key and the steering wheel in the golf swing. The arms act as the connecting rods and add some leverage to the swing. In the end, it is truly the hands that cause the body to coil and, in turn, the clubhead to swing. However, the body pivot needs to be understood and grooved through drill-work so that the body responds efficiently to the commands of the hands.

The body pivot can be broken up into two separate but connected sections:

1. The base pivot action of the hips against the knees and feet.
2. The shoulder turn of the backswing and downswing.

The basic image that the hips turn in a barrel will allow you to be more stable and to center your swing. Nevertheless, looking at hip turn in more detail and understanding all of the mechanics involved is going to increase your power, control, and consistency. For one, you must appreciate that during the backswing the right knee remains flexed but rotates slightly clockwise as the right hip turns back through the right heel and continues turning into the left heel. Also, the right hip sinks as the right thigh drops as if your were corkscrewing the hips into the ground. Ben Hogan, maybe the greatest ball striker who ever lived, was heard to say that when he practiced at Florida's Seminole Golf Club prior to the Masters each year, he felt his feet were sinking into the ground. He knew then that he was correctly coiling the hips. The turning of the hips gives a live coil to the legs and the base of the golf swing. There is live pressure in the left thigh all the way down to the ankle. When you're turning in the right way, the muscles in the right hip wind up like a spring.

The concept of the key (hands) turning on the rotor-motor (hips) to turn the axle (backbone) to spin the wheel (arms and clubshaft) underlies the principles involved in building a consistent backswing that sees the club swung correctly to Point A.

In describing the mechanics of the backswing in the most basic way, this is what happens: the hands move the hips, the hips turn the shoulders and swing the arms, and the swinging clubhead hinges the wrists. However, good golfers know a lot more is involved. So let me describe what I call the three "action zones."

Here, as the hands swing farther back and the right knee remains flexed, the right-hip turn increases.

Zone 1: The body coil happens early in the backswing, when the takeaway actions of the hands wind the hips against the knees and the feet, and the shoulders against the hips and arms.

At the start of the backswing, the hip turn transports the shoulders back. The shoulders turn as level as possible around the base of the neck. The left shoulder stays considerably higher than the right shoulder. The swinging clubhead completes the shoulder turn as it hinges the hands and swings the arms back and up.

Zone 2: The next loading action to occur comes from the centrifugal force and the momentum of the swinging clubhead. As the clubhead swings faster and past the hands, arms, and body, it causes the right wrist and right elbow to bend, the left wrist to cock. This swinging motion of the clubhead hinges the wrists correctly without any conscious action from the hands. Maintaining the pushing attitude in both hands causes the left arm to extend and the right arm to fold and load. As the clubhead hinges the wrist and bends the right arm, the left hand responds by pushing dynamically from the heel pad down and against the grip. The right hand increases its pushing action against the grip, also from the heel-pad wrist area as it pushes against the side of the clubshaft. This push loads the wrists and promotes the winding action of the muscles in the arms. There is also increased pressure in the hands that I see as a natural response similar to what would be experienced when swinging a hammer to hit a nail.

Zone 3: The momentum of the swinging club causes the arms to swing back and upward to a point as high as and in front of the right shoulder and arrive at a maximum coiled position.

At this point in the driver swing, the momentum of the swinging clubhead causes the left wrist to hinge automatically. Don't ever consciously cock the wrist.

There is no effort to lift the club with the hands and arms.

To develop a feel and confidence in the loading action of the backswing, start by swinging a sand iron at medium speed and employing the proper movements. The rag-doll approach of soft arms and shoulders will help you realize how much the swinging clubhead has to do with winding up on the backswing. It will also convince you that the famous golf instructor and author Ernest Jones was on track with his Swing the Clubhead concept.

I realize that no two players swing exactly the same, so I only look for three key positions when examining the backswing action of one of my students:

The hips have turned forty-five degrees.
The shoulders have turned ninety degrees.
The hands are opposite the right shoulder in
   height and depth.

When you arrive at Point A, the hips should be turned forty-five degrees and the shoulders ninety degrees. Also, the hands should be opposite the right shoulder in height and depth.

SWINGING DOWN TO POINT B

In reality, there is no pause at the top of the swing (Point A) and no division between the backswing and the downswing. The swing is one uninterrupted flowing motion.

The initial push-throw action of the downswing, seen from the front view (top) and the down-target view (bottom).

From this angle you can clearly see how the upper body is passive while the lower body is active. In swinging down, think of the upper body as a wall to push your hands away from, and keep pushing until your right arm fully straightens. This push-release swing helps you generate added clubhead speed and hit the ball more powerfully.

The downswing actually starts while the backswing is in progress, provided that the player has developed a true backswing motion—one that has the hands triggering hip movement, the hips triggering clubhead movement, and the movement of the clubhead loading the hands, arms, and shoulders.

The downswing should be triggered by throwing the clubhead with the hands in the direction of the ball. Think of the ball as the finish line to a race and your clubhead is your speeding car. If it's a tight race, you don't coast in. You put the pedal to the metal. It will feel as if you are releasing early in the downswing, but in actuality the angle between the clubshaft and your left arm will be retained late into the downswing. The result will be a pushing action with your hands extending the clubhead deep into the shot on the way to a full finish, up and over the left shoulder.

This pushing or throwing action uncocks the clubshaft,

Once the club reaches the hit zone, the upper body will move in behind the throw and start turning through the ball. This body-release action of the upper body allows you to accelerate the club even faster through impact.

so it lines up with the left arm as you drive the clubhead down and out toward the ball with the hands directing the action. The throw also causes the wrists to hinge back more initially because of the increase in pressure from the clubhead's resistance to acceleration. The effective mass of the clubhead increases as you accelerate the clubhead toward the ball.

Coming into the ball, you should feel that your upper body makes no active forward motion but only provides something for the hands and arms to push against and out from. Think of the upper body as part of a brick wall during the transition from backswing to downswing. The upper body will move in behind the push (throw) and be there when you need its force at impact and into the follow-through.

As the hands continue to push the clubhead in the direction of the ball, the left shoulder is forced upward, the right shoulder downward. This seesaw action of the shoulders supports the hands and arms in delivering the clubhead to the ball. This added loading of the wrists and right arm creates a winding-up effect, and power is unleashed once the hands complete the throw and reach the bottom of their downward motion near the ball.

The release means the unloading or unwinding of the stored power built up in the backswing and by the start-down action. Here's what involved:

The left arm and right upper arm move downward.
The right arm starts to straighten.
The shoulders rock.
The wrists uncock.

The hips unwind.
The left leg straightens.
The forearms rotate counterclockwise.

From the start of the downswing the action of the hands attempting to throw the clubhead toward the ball causes an increase in pressure in the wrist area. This increase in pressure corresponds to an increase in the effective mass in the club-head, as you exert an accelerating force on the club through the hands. After the initial throw, the clubhead goes from feeling very heavy to having virtually no effective mass. The hands must be very positive in continuing to exert force in driving the clubhead down and outward toward the ball. The wrists begin to fully uncock, and the right arm straightens and the rotation of the clubface comes into effect. This continuous rotation of the clubface by the hands promotes a full rotation of the hips and the forearms through the impact zone. This is truly a full releasing of all the stored-up power in the swing.

It is amazing how much the hips turn toward the target while the clubhead lags behind as you strike down and through the golf ball. The more thrust that is applied by the hands, the more the hips unwind at and through impact. The counterbalance action has the left hip turning and straighten-ing the left leg and moving the weight through the left heel and back into the right heel while the right hip remains the central axis point. This counterbalance action gives you the feeling that you have turned back into the right foot. Also, it gives you much more clearance through the impact area and allows for full extension of the club well into the follow-through. Once the left hip has fully cleared and the left leg has straightened, the right hip turns around the left hip's axis point. The right knee works in against the left knee and weight shifts fully off the right foot to be balanced fully on the left leg. These lower-body actions create the hula-hula action of the hips, allowing them to work as the motor and the counterbalance to the swinging clubhead.

If you look at impact not as a brief interval but as a zone of action, extending beyond the ball, it will give you a feeling of freedom. At the first moment of impact the hands are forced forward from their original address position. A line of sight from the eyes through the hands blocks out a position on the forward side of the big toe of the left foot. The wrists are level. The shoulders have rotated upward, again with the left shoulder high and the right shoulder low. The left hip is turned well through the ball. The left leg is straight or virtually straight. The body's weight is firmly in the ground through both feet. The hips are open to the target line.

There's more to impact for good players. Once the wrists fully uncock, the right arm makes a sidearm pitching action that helps your swing down and through on a more streamlined angle and creates a flat spot in the golf swing. In other words, the club, rather than making just a glancing blow, plows through the ball at high speed. The result: a stronger, straighter shot.

In the impact zone, you want the shoulders to return to a square position, parallel to the target line. By the end of impact, the left arm and clubshaft should line up. Upon completion of the impact interval, the back of the left hand and the palm of the right should be dead square to the target and rotating closed to the target line.

THE FOLLOW-THROUGH

The follow-through starts at the end of the impact zone (top) and continues until the clubshaft moves out of line with the left arm (bottom).

The follow-through starts at the end of the impact zone and continues until the clubshaft moves out of line with the left arm. Once the clubshaft moves out of line, the body-turn function loses its locked-in coordination with the hands and arms motion. The continuous pushing action of the hands releases the right shoulder, right hip, right knee, and right foot. It also causes the body to turn completely through the shot. The correct follow-through action keeps the hands, arms, and club in front of the body and does not allow the arms to collapse across the body as we move into the finish of the swing.

THE FINISH

The flow from follow-through into finish starts at the moment the clubhead moves out of line with the left arm as the wrists rehinge into the finish. The continuous action of uncocking and rotating the left hand adds to the momentum of the swinging clubhead. The momentum of the swinging clubhead and the arms carry the shoulders and hips fully through. The right shoulder passes the left, the hips turn fully counterclockwise, the right knee moves in more tightly against the left, and the right foot releases up to be balanced on the right toe. The left leg fully straightens and turns against the spikes underneath the left foot. The action is so fluid and rhythmic that you can only continue on freely, until you finally recoil. The complete unwinding action of the shoulders helps fully uncoil the hips and transfer weight to the left side until your body finally moves up to a balanced position. Your spine angle moves from the address position to a fully vertical position as you swing into a comfortable and relaxed finish position.

Here's what a balanced finish looks like.

CHAPTER 5

Croker's Four Cs

*Clubhead Speed, Center-Hit,
Control, and Consistency*

Practically every golfer I speak to cares little about anything but to be able to whip the driver into impact, make solid contact with the ball, and hit the shot at the target. I don't blame them one bit, because to paraphrase the great Ben Hogan: "Regardless of the importance of iron play, pitching, chipping, bunker play, and putting, if you can't drive the ball, you can't play golf."

Face it, there's no better feeling than hitting a tee shot far down the center of the fairway, especially when the swing is so effortless that you cannot really describe the sensation. When asked, most golfers simply say, "I felt nothing." This happens when you swing rhythmically and coordinate perfectly the movement of the body with the movement of the golf club.

One way to encourage a satisfying result is to make sure that you adhere to the address fundamentals I set forth in chapter 3. Another is to take every opportunity to watch PGA Tour professionals. The typical tour player's swing is so efficient that if you go to a tournament and watch any one of them hitting balls on the range, it will affect you positively. In fact, I know amateur golfers who have cured a slump by just watching the pros. Their supersmooth tempo, timing, and rhythm and good habits tend to rub off.

The other good ways to ensure that you drive the ball powerfully and accurately—and shoot low scores—are to generate high clubhead speed, hit the ball with the center of the clubface consistently, and control your shots like a pro. These abilities are all very much connected and a product of more precisely applying the new fundamentals and basic swing mechanics presented in the previous two chapters. Therefore, it is important to review the fine points that apply.

CLUBHEAD SPEED

If you have understood and applied the mechanics put forth thus far on the address, backswing, and downswing, you have already developed a good action. Well, now it's time to add a turbocharger in the change-of-direction area of the golf swing and show you how to increase the velocity of your downswing. One secret to accomplishing this goal is to realize that the hands are in fact quicker than the eyes. I want you to forget all the malarkey you have heard about watching the ball and waiting for the club. Instead, take control by throwing the clubhead downward toward the ball as fast as you can the split second you reach the top.

CENTER-HIT

As important as clubhead speed is to helping the golfer produce power, it is equally important to return the clubface squarely to the ball at impact. Clubhead speed must be correctly applied. That means that you must swing at the highest possible speed, while maintaining smooth rhythm and balance, and contact the back center portion of the ball with the center of the clubface, or sweet spot.

The direction of the throw is key, and in this department something can be learned from Sam Snead. Snead always claimed that when he wanted to hit an extralong drive, he made sure to start taking the club back a little slower than normal. What a slow, smooth start to the swing does is give you time to load the body, arms, and hands—to gather yourself at the top and put the club in the best possible position to throw from.

Some teaching methods call for a player to use the arms to thrust the club down into the ball. I disagree. It is far easier to hit the ball with the center of the clubface if you use your hands and wrists to control the action, just as you would when hammering a nail into a wall.

CONTROL

Another factor that is important to producing a square hit and accurate shot is realizing that when making your throw, you want the left arm and the clubshaft to line up at impact and the wrists to fully uncock. The clubshaft moving into line is the key to control because when you strive for this in-line position, you ensure that the clubface finishes dead square to the ball at impact. When the hands lag far behind the clubhead at impact, its face points well left of target, and when they finish well ahead of the clubhead, its face points right of target. Either way, the ball flies away from the direction of the target.

To learn the proper in-line actions of the downswing through impact, hit slow-motion chip shots. Start by uncocking the hands so that the clubshaft moves in line with the left arm by the time the hands reach the impact area. Continue pushing, maintaining that straight-line relationship until you have fully turned the hips and shoulders and are in a balanced position. Next, gradually add speed to the chip motion and hit balls. Graduate to the driver once you feel confident about matching the correct in-line movements with the shorter clubs.

CONSISTENCY

In the most simple terms, knowing what to do and how to do it are the secrets to consistency. The only way to truly evolve into a more consistent player and be able to return the center of the clubface squarely to the ball a high percentage of the time is through practice. Not casual practice, just "beating balls" as I call it, but by hard and honest practice using the following drills to perfect your address, backswing, and downswing.

Address
Doorway Drill

Purpose: To help you learn and groove a solid setup that promotes a consistently good golf swing.

What to Do: Place your left heel (ankle area) up against the

The Doorway Drill will train you to tilt your left hip up higher than the right. Once you groove this setup position, you will find it easier to make a free backswing and turn through the ball on the downswing.

edge of a doorframe and set your right foot down as shown in the photograph above. Turn both feet outward slightly.

Next, bend from the hips making sure that your pelvis tilts up and forward slightly so there is no hollow in the small of the back. Slide your left hip to the left until your left thigh rests against the doorframe and you feel that the left hip is higher than the right hip. Bend the knees out toward the toes but keep your body weight evenly balanced across the soles of your feet.

Let your arms hang down naturally with the hands positioned in the center of your body. Extend the left arm, let the right elbow bend slightly, and set the left shoulder higher than the right.

Backswing

Swivel Chair–Desk Drill

Purpose: To help you feel how the body responds to the hands in the swing.

The Swivel Chair–Desk Drill teaches you to feel the benefit of a pushing action on the backswing.

What to Do: Sit in a swivel chair at your desk with your feet a few inches off the ground. Push gently against the desk (to the left) with your right hand and note how your body turns clockwise. This is what happens automatically once you trigger the swing by employing a pushing action.

Shaft Drill

Purpose: To help you learn the benefits of a press-action swing trigger and how to spring-load the backswing.

What to Do—Step One: Stick the end of a shaft a couple of inches into the ground behind the ball, then take your address.

The Shaft Drill: step one.

The Shaft Drill: step two.

Step Two: Press the hands forward. Notice how the hips turn, the left leg starts to straighten, weight moves through the left heel and into the right heel. Note too how the shoulders tilt due to your hand action and turning hips.

The Shaft Drill: step three.

Step Three: Start the backswing by pushing the left hand straight back against the slightly resisting right hand.

The Shaft Drill: step four.

Step Four: Continue to push back with the left hand until the left wrist bends slightly and the hips and shoulders turn even more powerfully. Keep pushing until the shaft is released out of the ground and starts accelerating past the hands. The more you push and turn, the more you spring-load the backswing.

Downswing

Break-the-Barrier Drill

Purpose: This drill helps you feel the resistance in the swing, between the body and the hands. Again, the body makes no active forward motion but only provides something to push against and out from. Power is derived from having a position you can maintain. If you can't hold your position in a debate, you lose the argument. Look at large electric generators. It is the huge bolts securing them to the ground that give

The Break-the-Barrier Drill will train you to let the momentum of the hands pull the body up to a full finish when swinging a club.

the armature something to turn against and hence generate power. If you tried to push a refrigerator on roller skates, how much power do you think you could generate?

What to Do: Without a club, "freeze" your body at the top of the backswing position. Do not allow your body to move at all throughout this part of the exercise.

Now, with your arms and hands as relaxed as possible, uncock your hands directly at where the ball would be, but don't let them go past an imaginary barrier in front of your left thigh, your body staying in the top-of-the-backswing position. Feel the blood rushing to your fingertips. Do this until it is drilled into your muscle memory.

Repeat this procedure, but after impact allow the momentum of your hands to break through the imaginary barrier and pull the body up to a full finish. Drill this in with a really aggressive swing.

Now you can take some full practice swings with a club, retaining the feeling you have acquired. Finally, hit some balls while focusing on that feeling.

Uncocking Drill

Purpose: This backyard drill helps you learn the uncocking action of the left wrist. Further, it teaches you the in-line position of the left wrist and forearm that makes for square and powerful impact.

What to Do: Grip down six to ten inches on the club's handle with the left hand only.

Swing the club back to a point level with your waist. During this part of the drill, the hands, arms, and club should be in front of the body.

Uncock the left wrist (thumb moving in a downward direction), so the grip end of the club makes contact under the left forearm just to the inside of the bone, and the club-shaft and left arm move into a straight-line position.

The Uncocking Drill, which can be practiced in your own back-yard, trains you to line the left arm up with the clubshaft when swinging through impact.

Propeller Drill

Purpose: To alleviate tension in the arms and shoulders and help you develop a down-and-out swing path.

What to Do: Swing a short iron to the top. Next, throw the

The Propeller Drill trains you to make a free and powerful hands-release of the club. Just look at that clubshaft shimmering!

clubhead at the ball while resisting with the body and uncocking the wrists. Feel how the arms swing freely up and the clubhead releases fully. Notice too how much clubhead speed is generated.

A-to-B Drill

Purpose: This drill, best done in slow motion, teaches the hands how to direct the club on the correct path to the ball using a pushing action. It also teaches the hands to uncock correctly so that the clubshaft moves in line with the left arm through impact—Point B. Further, it trains the hands to push the club rhythmically, so that the release of the hips and shoulders is perfectly timed and the club's face strikes the ball solidly, sending the ball to the target.

What to Do—Stage One: Throw the club down toward the ball, stopping when the hands reach a point opposite the right foot. Here, the clubshaft should be in line with the left arm while the clubface should point outward.

Stage Two: Push your right hand against your left hand in the direction of the ball.

Stage Three: The right side releases, with the right knee touching the left knee. The hips turn fully against the feet and both heels are heavy in the ground. The turning action of the hips causes a faster rate of release of the clubface.

Stage Four: Both wrists fully uncock and the hips continue turning as the club is delivered into the ball. At this point, the shoulders are parallel to the target line, the left leg is straight, and the left arm and clubshaft line up again.

Stage Five: Repeat, adding speed gradually.

Stage Six: Hit balls and graduate to driver.

*The A-to-B Drill teaches the hands to swing the club correctly
from Point A (top) down to Point B (bottom).*

CHAPTER 6

Technical High Points

*Reviewing the Critical Elements
of the Setup and Swing Will Help
You Keep Playing Good Golf*

If you can remember back to the days of your early child-hood when you first learned to write the letters of the alpha-bet, it was not all that easy. First you learned to print each let-ter, then you learned to write the alphabet in script, then how to tie all the letters together into words. Finally, you learned how to employ those words in sentences, in paragraphs, in a story. If you recall, what made everything easier was repeti-tion. This required discipline and dedication, but the harder you worked, the simpler things got. In fact, in a relatively short time you probably learned how to develop good pen-manship without even thinking about it. You were on auto-matic pilot and still are today.

The same philosophy that applies in the aforesaid story

applies to golf. You must work hard to learn the right skills, from the most basic to the most sophisticated, then take the time to review them over and over, mentally and physically, so that you understand the swing intellectually and can play by feel too. Only then will you be able to more consistently repeat a good setup and swing and be able to find your swing again quickly if you fall into a slump.

Although I have tried to keep things as simple as possible in the first five chapters, I want to be sure that my instructional message comes through loud and clear and that you are confident that you can apply the swing principles I have put forth. To make sure of this, I am going to review the technical high points mentioned so that you can have these at your fingertips when you are ready to begin a regular practice regimen or when you experience a bad patch and want to recall information right away.

What follows are instructional photographs with short captions explaining things we have talked about previously for you to go over when you feel up to it. Call this a wrap-up, call this a refresher course, it doesn't really matter. What matters is that you take the time to visualize each and every move in your mind's eye, and then physically repeat the movement of the setup or swing on the practice tee. Ben Hogan and Bobby Jones did this, Jack Nicklaus and Arnold Palmer did this too during their heydays, Tiger Woods does it. Practice may not make perfect, but it does give you the best chance of repeating a good swing. And when you do that, you hit more accurate shots, shoot lower scores, and enjoy the game of golf even more.

Take Dead Aim

Before swinging, it's critical that you stare intently at the target to get a feel for distance and the shot at hand.

See the Target, Feel the Target

Before stepping fully into the shot, set the clubface down square to the ball and target.

The Setup Determines the Motion

Setting the feet, knees, hips, and shoulders parallel to the target line gives you the best chance of hitting an accurate shot.

Perfect Posture

At address, the pelvis should tilt up, and there should be a minimal arch in your lower back.

Good Grip

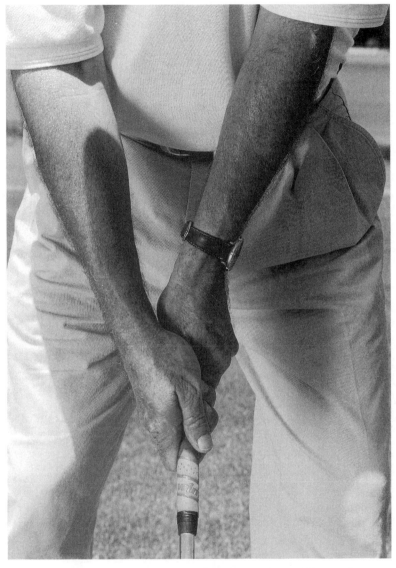

When gripping the club, be sure that the Vs formed by each hand's thumb and forefinger parallel each other.

Rehearsal Time

Slowly waggling the club away from the target will help you physically rehearse the correct hand and arm motion for the upcoming swing.

Push, Don't Pull

It's critical that you practice the push-action used in the Path to Better Golf swing. Remember, for best results, the left hand should push against a resisting right hand.

Use Your Imagination

To help you swing correctly to Point A, imagine a good player in the at-the-top position, preferably Ben Hogan.

Aussie Action

My fellow Aussie Greg Norman still swings powerfully into impact, Point B, because he pushes the club through with his hands. So should you.

Extend Yourself

When swinging down, concentrate on extending the club to the end of the impact zone and you will increase clubhead speed and make solid contact with the ball at Point B.

Putting Practice Pays Off

Practicing putting is a shortcut to learning the pushing action of the big swing.

Chip-Shot Practice Is Well Worth the Time and Effort

Practicing chipping teaches you to feel the relationship between hand movement and body rotation, and promotes "educated hands" to build the full swing on.

Cross the Finish Line

Holding a good finish for a few seconds, during practice, will allow you to feel the various correct body and club positions, so that you are more apt to "push" into them the next time you play.

INDEX

consistency, 24, 55–57
  secrets to, 98
control of shot, 97–98

delayed hit, 12
Doorway Drill, 98–100
down-and-out swing path, 108
downswing, 12–16
  clubface in, 17, 87, 89
  clubhead in, 12–14, 17, 50, 87, 88, 89
  clubshaft in, 87–88
  drills, 105–10
  faults, 48–50
  hand movement in, 21, 50, 53, 87, 88, 89
  hip movement in, 51–52, 89–90
  impact zone and, 53, 89, 122
  increasing velocity of, 96
  legs and, 50, 89, 90
  push-throw action of, 48–49, 85
  release, 89–90
  tips, 21
  transition from backswing to, 48–49, 84–86
draw, 17, 53
drills
  address, 98–100
  backswing, 100–104
  chipping, 33–35
  downswing, 105–10
  playing by feel, 33
  push-action, 5, 109–10
  throwing action, 14–16
drive, four components of, 95–98
driver, 83, 98, 109
Duval, David, 51

Earp, Charlie, xxvi
elbows, in forward press, 73
eyes on ball, 51, 73

fades, 17, 53
fat shot, 50
faults, 10–11
  backswing, 41, 42
  downswing, 48–49

feet position
  in address routine, 61, 70, 71
  body alignment and, 62
  in downswing release, 89, 90
  in finish, 92
  in putting, 19
  in setup position, 6, 7
  in waggle, 73
  weight balance and, 61
finish, 54, 92–93, 125
follow-through, 91–92
forearms. See arms
forward press
  address movement to, 10
  into backswing, 20, 42, 73–75
  chipping and, 22
  hand movement creating, 4, 8, 11–12, 73
  left hand movement following, 4
  push-action and, 3

Golf My Way (Nicklaus), 55–56
Graham, David, xxvi, 32
grip, 117
  in address, 58, 64–69
  for putting, 19
  See also hand position
Grout, Jack, 56

hand movements
  alignment and, 62
  in backswing, 11–12, 20, 39, 40, 41, 45, 81, 82
  in backswing-to-downswing transaction, 48–49, 50
  in body pivot, 80, 81
  Break-the-Barrier Drill, 105–6
  in chipping, 22–23, 124
  control of shot and, 97–98
  in downswing, 21, 50, 53, 87, 88, 89
  drill for directing club on correct path, 109–10
  drill for pushing action of backswing, 100–101
  follow-through, 92
  forward press, 4, 8, 11–12, 73

Marsh, Graham, xxvi

neck injury avoidance, 50
Nicklaus, Jack, 21, 50, 55–56, 112
Norman, Greg, 121

off-center hits, spine angle and, 54
off-line shots, avoidance of, 38, 42,
    79
open stance, 7

Palmer, Arnold, 112
pelvis upward tilt, 6, 60, 116
PGA Tour. *See* professional golfers
pitching wedge, 24
pitch shots, xxvii, 18, 24–26
pivot action, 78–84
    reverse, 45
Player, Gary, xxvi, 32
posture, 54, 60–61, 71, 116
    spine alignment, 5, 54, 60, 92
professional golfers
    chipping style, 22
    clubface through impact and, 53
    consistency of, 55–57, 98
    downswing and, 50
    efficiency of swing, 96
    free head movement and, 51
    as personal golf-approach models,
        31–33, 120
    setup and, 55–57
    See also specific names
Propeller Drill, 108–9
pulling action, 8–9, 17
pull slice, 49
push-action, 119, 121
    in backswing, 8–12, 39, 71, 82
    in downswing, 14, 17, 48–49, 53,
        85–88
    drill, 5, 109–10
    follow-through, 92
    importance of, xxvii, 3, 4, 32
    putt push-and-resist practice for,
        18, 20, 123
putting, 18–21
    backswing tips, 20
    downswing tips, 21
    object of, 18

as push-action practice, 18, 20, 123
    setup tips, 19
    in swing sequence, xxvii, 18

Queensland Sunshine Circuit, xxvi

release, 88–90
reverse pivot, 45
right arm, in downswing, 88, 90
right hand
    in backswing, 82
    in early stage of swing, 39
    in foreward press, 4, 8, 11
    grip, 66, 67–68
    in takeaway, 78
right wrist, impact and, 52–53
rotation. *See* body rotation
rotor-motor backswing, 9–12
Royal Melbourne Golf Club, xxv
Runyan, Paul, xxvi, 22

St. Andrews (Scotland), 1
sand iron, 24, 83
Sandringham Golf Links (Australia),
    xxv
setup
    doorway drill, 98–100
    of Nicklaus, 55–57
    position, 6–7, 115
    in putting, 19
    target line imagery, 59
    tips, 19
    See also address
Shaft Drill, 101–4
shape of shot, 17
short irons
    Propeller Drill, 108
    stance and, 7
    swing technique and, 9
shoulders
    in address, 60, 62
    in backswing, 9–11, 41, 42, 45, 80,
        81, 82, 84
    in downswing, 50, 80, 88
    during finish, 92
    forward press and, 4, 73
    in impact zone, 54, 90
    in putting setup position, 19